Home-Alone Kids

Home-Alone Kids

The Working Parent's Complete Guide to
Providing the Best Care for Your Child

Bryan E. Robinson

Bobbie H. Rowland

Mick Coleman

Lexington Books

D.C. Heath and Company • Lexington, Massachusetts • Toronto

Library of Congress Cataloging-in-Publication Data

Robinson, Bryan E.
Home-alone kids : the working parent's complete guide to providing
the best care for your child / by Bryan E. Robinson, Bobbie H.
Rowland, Mick Coleman.
p.   cm.
Includes index.
ISBN 0–669–19504–9 (alk. paper)
1.   Latchkey children—United States.   2.   Child rearing—United
States.   I.   Rowland, Bobbie H.   II.   Coleman, Mick.   III. Title.
HQ777.65.R628   1989
649'.1—dc19   88–31392

Published simultaneously in Canada
Printed in the United States of America
Casebound International Standard Book Number: 0–669–19504–9
Library of Congress Catalog Card Number: 88–31392

The paper used in this publication meets
the minimum requirements of American National Standard
for Information Sciences—Permanence of Paper
for Printed Library Materials, ANSI Z39.48.1984.

88 89 90 91 92 8 7 6 5 4 3 2 1

For my mother,
Shirley Thompson Robinson,
who always did her best to ensure my nurturance,
and care—B.E.R.

For
Molly and Patrick,
my grand(est) children, who at their earliest ages show
promise of becoming self-reliant and autonomous—B.H.R.

For
Chrystal and Sherry,
whose care for others has helped to create a safer and
more nurturing society—M.C.

Contents

Preface

I F we could wave a magic wand, every child would have a safe and stimulating home environment with a caring adult present at all times. We believe, ideally, that children should always be supervised by responsible adults whether at school, home, or play. But today there are many situations in which children find themselves home alone without adult supervision because their parents have no alternatives.

It is estimated that as many as seven million children care for themselves at home alone daily. For the purposes of this book a *home-alone child* or *self-care child* is one who has the responsibility of caring for himself or herself in an unsupervised setting on a regular basis. For some children the time spent in self-care is short and relatively stress-free. For others it entails the care of brothers and sisters, being alone for long hours, and having untold fears and apprehensions.

Some children enjoy self-care and develop independence and self-reliance. They are trusted to make reasonable decisions and do perfectly fine when left home alone. Others simply cannot handle the pressures of self-care and are overwhelmed with rules and responsibilities. This book is addressed to parents who have no alternatives to self-care arrangements for their children.

Chapter 1 is about kids at home alone and will help you decide if this arrangement is for you. Many children are in well-planned, secure situations. One of the first things you will do is examine your own attitudes and feelings about home-alone care. We give you some help with the Self-Care Security Quiz. This test will be the starting point of your examination of all aspects of self-care and what it means to leave your child home alone.

In chapter 2 we propose eight critical questions that you must answer before deciding on home-alone care for your child. You will be encouraged to consider your child's age and maturity level as major components. Other aspects you will need to think about are amount of preparation, location of your home, community resources, amount of time your child is left alone, and type of check-in system you will use in your absence. You can decide if your child has a high-risk or low-risk rating for self-care by computing your child's score on the **HART,** which stands for Home-Alone Risk Test.

In chapter 3 we show you, step by step, how to create a safe, reliable self-care arrangement once you have made your decision. We offer suggestions that serve as checks and balances between preparation and protection. We offer ideas for making the best of your home-alone care. Safety is stressed and developing an after-school schedule for your child is just one of the helpful tips included.

In the fourth chapter we address various ways of monitoring your child's adjustment to self-care once it is under way. We identify signs of stress and behavior changes that need immediate attention. We have relied heavily on interviews with children to give a full picture of what it means to be home alone daily. We make several suggestions for helping your child adjust.

Chapter 5 takes a realistic look at balancing your work and family life as you meet the challenges of parenting in the twenty-first century. No one said being a working parent was going to be easy and being a home-alone child is not always easy, either. We talk about parent-child relationships and the importance of spending quality time together. We encourage you to plan carefully for those important hours that you and your child have together.

If you find self-care is not working, you will learn of other care arrangements that will fit your situation better in chapter 6. Choosing a program is important. We have identified programs and options for your investigation, and we have included a guide to help you select the best.

Chapter 7 provides a knapsack, so to speak, filled with ideas and suggestions that will help you bolster your child's self-care arrangement. Included are lists of books for adults and children, after-school programs, hotlines, safety hints, fun activities for parents and children to do together, self-care preparation programs, organizations, magazines, and much, much more.

We have dedicated our energies to alerting parents and professionals to the importance of safe and stimulating environments for kids. Being home alone does not have to be destructive or devastating, but it does have to be carefully orchestrated. We reach out to all the children who need our best thoughts and actions as we plan for their care. We believe parents want to do what is best for their children; they want to open the door of opportunity as wide as possible. Our goal is to offer you, the parent, a key to this door in hope that it will ultimately unlock many doors for you and your family.

Acknowledgments

W e gratefully acknowledge our many friends, colleagues, and family members who have helped make this book a reality. We especially appreciate the steadfast personal and administrative support of Dr. Mary Thomas Burke and Dr. Harold H. Heller. We give special thanks to the following people for contributing case material for the book: Ruchi Mathur, Kapila Mathur, Joy Morrison, Maureen O'Bryan, Hassie Short, Phyllis Gryder, Millie Gutherie, Mary Witherington, June Kirby, Nickey Chaney, Barbara Jordan, Swaim Strong, Nancy Ratliff, Barbara Williams, and Sara Kelly Hanes. We also benefited from the help of Sandra Sparks and the use of her "Boredom Busters" and other ideas from "The Key to Being on My Own." Special appreciation is extended to Barbara Jordan, Joyce Green, and Lauren Stayer for their tireless efforts in manuscript preparation.

We thank the staff and our editor, Margaret Zusky, at Lexington Books, whose excitement, creativity, and belief in this project helped us get many manuscript drafts into print. Last, but not least, we thank all the anonymous home-alone children who shared their lives with us and the parents we talked with who are doing such a good job with the delicate balance between home and work.

1

Should You Leave
Your Child Home Alone?

S INGLE mother Barbara Jordan, of Raleigh, N.C., has two sons, one
five and the other eleven. Her boys are among the approximately
seven million children equipped with keys to their homes. They are
home alone before and after school without adult supervision. "It's not
my first choice, but it's the only thing I can afford," says Barbara. "As
soon as I get to work in the morning, I call my older son who is responsible for getting himself and his younger brother off to school. In the
afternoons they must call me as soon as they get home. They are not
allowed to leave the house or to use any electrical appliances, not even
television. Although I constantly worry about them, my oldest seems
to have developed a lot of responsibility from the experience. Even
though it's working pretty good, I still feel guilty sometimes and
wonder if I'm doing the right thing."

Barbara Jordan's uncertainty about her children's self-care arrangement is typical of the parents we have talked to. They express pride in
their children's ability to assume responsibility in the home, but they
feel guilty about asking their children to assume responsibility at such
a young age. Despite her uncertainty, Barbara remains upbeat: "I want
everything to be perfect, and I'm hoping to strike a happy medium. I
try to be careful that I don't take my frustrations out on my sons. It's
important that I actually hear what my kids say to me. Sometimes,
though, I must admit it's hard making all the decisions between the
kids, the job, and the home."

Have you agonized over whether to leave your child home alone? Are you afraid your child will have an accident or an emergency in your absence? Do you fear your child will be emotionally scarred for life from the fear of being alone? Do you trust your child enough to stick to the rules you agreed upon? If you're thinking about leaving your child at home alone while you work, or if your child is already in self-care, this book is for you. Regardless of your child's age, being alone in the morning or afternoon for just one hour is a big step—for your child and for you as a parent. But you are not alone. The numbers of children home alone jumped during the 1970s and 1980s when economic trends led to increases in the number of families in which both parents work. The large number of divorces also led to single-parent households and record numbers of women as sole wage earners. A 1982 estimate by the United States Department of Labor put the number of children ten years of age and younger who care for themselves when not in school at seven million.

Are Latchkey Kids Really "Corner Crouchers"?

You have probably heard the term "latchkey kids," referring to children at home alone. Negative associations with this term were carried over from the eighteenth century, when "latchkey" referred to the method of lifting the door latch to gain access into homes. By the turn of the century in the United States, latchkey kids were called "dorks" because they had their own door keys to get inside their homes. During the 1940s, keys around a child's neck signaled poverty, neglect, and lack of motherly love and affection.

Because of this negative carryover in the 1980s, it has become common practice to steer away from that term. Most children in self-care are not deprived or neglected, and their working parents try to provide the very best for their kids. Still, you may have read myths about latchkey kids in popular magazines and newspapers. Parents tell us of horror stories that make them feel afraid and guilty for leaving their children by themselves. We have talked to many parents who tearfully share their concerns that their children face serious social and emotional damage as a result of being home alone. These worries are fueled by grim stories in magazines, newspapers, television, and some consumer books. You may have seen pictures of tattered waifs with keys around their necks or fearful children cowering in closets. Such titles as "Yes We Are Afraid and We Are Lonely" or "Latchkey Blues: When Kids Come Home" typify the hysteria that adds to parents' concerns and guilt. Some publications capitalize on the potential dangers in latchkey situations for reader appeal. They manufacture factless and emotional conclusions.

Some popular stereotypes are that home-alone children:

- are being hurried to grow up too fast too soon.
- face serious social and emotional damage from being left alone.
- are more sexually active than adult-supervised kids.
- get bad grades in school and do poorly on standardized tests.
- feel negatively about themselves and their relationships with others.
- have more fears, anxieties, and insecurities than children who have one parent at home.
- get into more trouble and have less self-control than children with a parent at home.

Most popularized accounts describe only a handful of the seven million children at home alone and present negative stereotypes of these youngsters. They misrepresent the scientific facts through what we call *latchkeyphobia*—exaggerated fear of placing children in self-care. As a parent reading these exaggerations, you may wonder what kind of permanent damage your child suffers at the cost of your working full-time. If you read these stereotypes and are fearful and guilty for having or even thinking about having self-care arrangements, then you have *latchkeyphobia*.

Good News about Latchkey Kids

Staying home alone is a grownup responsibility that some say has intellectual, social, and emotional side effects. But no study has ever found any truth to the stereotypes that conjure up images of delinquent, neglected youngsters. In fact, quite the opposite is true. New studies show that all is not bad for kids who stay home alone. Previous reports of psychological harm to home-alone children are based on studies done in urban, high-crime areas. When researchers turn their attention to suburban and rural children, both black and white, with both blue- and white-collar parents, the findings are quite different. For every study reporting negative effects on children in self-care, a comparable study can be cited that discounts these negative claims. The latest studies find no differences between self-care children and supervised children on self-esteem, self-reliance, academic achievement, social adjustment, fear of being alone, identity, and sense of control of their lives.

There are even indications that children in self-care are more mature and self-reliant than children under the watchful eye of an adult. Merlyn Woods' study of 108 supervised and unsupervised fifth-grade children in Philadelphia shows that children given responsibilities at home score higher on school achievement tests than children without household chores. Mothers employed full time and away for large portions of their child's day have children with the best social adjustment and intelligence scores. Children whose mothers work at home or who are away part time do not do as well.

Psychologist Deborah Vandell, at the University of Texas, compared children in self-care with those in day care centers. Her findings reveal that teachers rate day care school-age children more poorly on work and study skills than home-alone children. Peers also view day care children more negatively than self-care kids.

Although these studies point out positive aspects of self-care, we still don't know if self-care builds self-reliance or if parents select their most self-reliant children for self-care and place their less mature kids with a sitter or in a day care center. But we do know one thing: being left alone while Mom works doesn't always have the harmful effects that we see and hear about on television or read about in the press. Harm-free and secure self-care arrangements work when parents follow the guidelines in this book.

Home-Alone Kids Speak Out

We call latchkey kids of the 1980s home-alone kids. They are not, for the most part, eating cold meals, neglected or deprived of their parent's love and affection, or pushed out of the nest before they can fly. We rarely hear about successful self-care experiences, but they do exist. Many children are in well-planned, secure arrangements. Twelve-year-old Marc, for example, stays home alone each day after school for two hours until his parents get off work. During that time, he does his homework and watches television. In an emergency, he knows to contact his grandmother, who lives nearby. His parents have set two rules he must follow: don't turn on the oven and complete homework before watching television. Marc says he follows these rules, which he sees as fair, enjoys being alone, and is never afraid.

Tommy and Terri are learning to be home alone and feel good about it:

> This is the first year that my sister and I have taken care of ourselves after school. I'm ten years old and she's eight. We live two blocks from school and can cut across yards and be home in five minutes. Mostly everything is going good. We have rules and we have to do our homework whenever we get home. Sometimes there's a mix-up and my sister's late or it's raining or it's soccer game day and I get confused. To make it worse, I even cried one afternoon because I didn't know if we should wait for the neighbor to pick us up. You see, it was raining—not very hard—and I couldn't remember if we walk when it's a little rain or ride with the neighbor. My teacher has tried to help me by going over what I'm supposed to do just before school is out. They all brag about me and tell me how smart I am to take care of my sister, but I can tell you sometimes my stomach hurts. Last week my stomach hurt three mornings. I went to school but my stomach hurt all day. Mom's helping me to remember by giving me a list each morning. If there's a change in plans, she calls school and talks directly to me. I want to stay at home because I was too big to go to day care. Mostly they did things for little kids. I like to ride my bike and watch T.V. When my stepsister comes home—she's eighteen—at 4:00 p.m., she lets me ride and play outside and she takes care of my sister. I'll soon be eleven, and Mom thinks that's a good age to become responsible. And so do I!

Scott also says he enjoys being alone after school:

> My name is Scott. I'm eleven years old, and I live outside a small town. My dad gets me up in the mornings, and then he and my mom leave for work at six o'clock. I watch TV until seven o'clock; then I get ready for school and leave at seven-thirty. I get

home from school at four o'clock and my parents at about five o'clock. It's quiet where I live, and my neighbors are very close. Some are at home in the afternoons, and some are not. I've never lost my key because I keep it in my pocket. I've done this for two or three years. I've never been scared, either. I like getting home first. It makes me feel bigger—like I can do something by myself. Oh yeah, sometimes I hear things and get a little scared. But anybody would do that—even a grownup. Anyway, I've never had a real problem, except when the school bus was late, and I called my mom. I've learned that Mom and Dad can trust me.

Twelve-year-old Ruchi Mathur talks openly about the pros and cons of her single mother's real-estate job and how it takes her mother away from home a lot:

When I get home from school at four, I usually have a key to get in if Mom's not here. I usually get a snack, eat it, start watching TV, and do my homework. About six or seven my mom usually gets home. Sometimes she'll get food ready for dinner, and sometimes she'll call me and tell me to make the food. My older sister [15] babysits on Tuesdays, Wednesdays, and Thursdays so I'm by myself on those days. She gets home at five-thirty. It's sort of scary because you're sitting there by yourself, so I talk on the telephone a lot. Mom gets mad at me for talking on the phone so much. Sometimes when it gets dark and she's not here, my sister and me both get scared. Sometimes you hear these weird noises, you know? Like when it's windy, you can hear the screen rattling, especially when it's dark. You wonder if there could be burglars outside or something. In the daytime I don't really mind being by myself, but at night I have to have somebody here, either my sister or my mom. I think it's fun when Mom is gone 'cause I get to do the things I want to do. She doesn't mind if I have friends over as long as we don't mess up the house, and sometimes we walk around the block. But we can't leave the neighborhood. When she's here she says, "Get off the telephone, do your homework." I miss her a lot because she's not here half the time. I just wish she would be home more often. And sometimes she's not here for dinner and if she is, you have to hurry up and eat because she has to go for an appointment. I'm used to it. I want her to get married because I want a dad too, because dads will take you places. I wish she would get back together with my dad, but he's remarried now. He never calls us anymore. I'm mad 'cause he never writes or anything either. I wish he was here. I just think it would be lots more fun having two parents. Sometimes when Mom comes home late, she goes upstairs and works in her office. She's working all the time. She's always on the phone and we don't ever get to talk. When parents come home, they should be with their kids and talk to them a lot, watch TV with them, and spend as much time as you can with them 'cause they're not going to be there a lot. My mom doesn't listen to radio or watch TV because she's always working and doesn't know any of the songs I like or TV shows I like. If we're talking about a song we like, she says, "What are you listening to?" She doesn't like it. She doesn't know what's "in" or nothing. If she was home more, she'd watch TV and listen to radio more and she'd know what we like and understand us more. She'd know who Motley Crue is. My mom got mad because I got my report card and made a "C." She put me on restriction for a long time, and I wanted to run away. One "C" is not all that bad. It's average. My mom wants me to be the perfect child and it's hard. She wants me to be perfect, and I'm just average. I know she cares but sometimes it feels like she doesn't because she's not here hardly any. Sometimes I think, gosh, what a mom. But she has to work, 'cause my dad's not here. I understand that, and she brings in lots of money. It's fun most of the time, but it's scary sometimes. And I miss her a lot because she's not hardly ever here. Even though there's good and bad to being home alone, overall it's about even.

Your Biggest Worries

The most worry is generated not by the children but by concerned parents who want to provide the best while earning the family's income. A more accurate popularly portrayed version of self-care arrangements might be the nail-biting parent crouched in a corner rather than the child. Parents often have more difficulty adjusting to self-care arrangements than their kids.

We know from our own contact with more than eighteen hundred parents that fear, guilt, embarrassment, and uncertainty are common reactions to having children at home alone. Because of the historical negative stigma associated with latchkey kids, some parents are ashamed to admit to having made such arrangements. They are afraid others will think they don't care about their kids. Although they routinely leave their children without adult supervision, they try to hide it. They never tell even their own parents, much less business associates.

The Three O'Clock Syndrome

"No Missy, you cannot go over to Mandy's house. You know the rules. This is not the place or the time to change our agreement. Hold on, honey, I have a call on another line."

"Sirls, Burns, and Cantrell Associates. Ms. Patterson speaking. No, I'm sorry. He's out of town until Monday. Yes, I certainly will. Thank you for calling."

"Missy, now where were we? Oh yes, I'm counting on you to keep your end of the bargain. Have you done your homework and straightened your room? Why is your brother screaming? Honey, please try to get along. No, I'm not blaming you. He's just younger than you are, and I depend on you to watch after him. Sweetheart, I have another call. I have to go. Do your homework and fix your brother a snack. I'll take you to Burger King tonight for being such a good girl and doing such a good job. I love you."

"Sirls, Burns, and Cantrell Associates."

Does that conversation sound familiar? It happens so frequently around the United States everyday that it has been given a name: "Three o'clock syndrome." It occurs as uneasy parents interrupt their work to call home and check on their kids. During this time, businesses report productivity slowdowns, increases in assembly-line accidents, and absenteeism. There may be as many as two or three calls each afternoon. Sometimes the calls come in from children checking in with their working parents.

Ten-year-old Heather comes home from school, unlocks her front door, and secures it behind her. She calls her mother at work to tell her she is home safe and spends the next two hours completing homework until her mother gets home. "We have strict rules that Heather must follow when she's home alone," her mother says. "She knows that she is not to allow strangers or friends inside when I'm not home. She has a routine that she follows every afternoon so I feel pretty secure about that. I think being alone for a few hours a day makes her more self-reliant and responsible. But I must admit that I worry about her constantly."

Parents have every reason to be concerned when their children are home alone. But it is important to put exaggerated concerns into perspective. Self-care does not necessarily hurt a child's development. There are many different kinds of self-care arrangements. Some work; some don't. Some are healthy; others are not. The range is broad. Some children in self-care are alone at home, and some are supervised by an older brother or sister. Some children are supervised *in absentia* by parents through telephone calls, while others have no communication with adults. Many home-alone kids are on their own but stop by a friend's house where no adults are present or hang out in the local shopping mall or convenience store. Others check in with a neighbor before playing with friends in the neighborhood.

Reports from different parts of the country tell of problems with children who hang out in the public library while their parents are working. Children have burdened library staff with discipline problems they have neither the time nor the training to handle. The Los Angeles County Library System had trouble in its forty-two sites with as many as three hundred to four hundred children hanging out among the stacks while their parents worked. The problem is that these children are not there to study or read. They're looking for something to do and have nowhere else to go. In some cases their working parents have told them to stay in the library after school because they consider it a haven. A librarian in one large city witnessed a child run down by a car as the little girl raced across a busy street in pursuit of her older brother who had been left in charge of her. Other librarians have reported cases of abductions, fistfights, and other disruptions.

It is difficult to talk about self-care being good or bad, since there are so many kinds of arrangements. Researcher Laurence Steinberg found that these different types of arrangements can make a difference in children's adjustment. His study of 865 fifth- through ninth-graders in a suburban area of Madison, Wis., revealed that, with respect to self-reliance, identity, and susceptibility to peer pressure, self-care children who reported home after school and had *in absentia* parental supervision (set rules or parent's telephone calls) were no different from those who were supervised by their parents at home after school. But when children "hung out" at a friend's house (where no adults were home) or on the street, they were at higher risk of getting into trouble. Steinberg concluded that the differences in the settings where self-care takes place—not simply whether the child is in a self-care arrangement or under adult supervision—are the most critical factors in the child's adjustment.

Workable self-care arrangements depend upon many factors that we will cover: parent's attitude, age and readiness of the child to be left alone, the youngster's preparation for self-care, safety of the child's neighborhood, available community resources, how long the child is alone, and type of supervision (or lack of it). There is a good deal of controversy surrounding the question of preparing children for self-care. But for parents like Barbara Jordan, for whom adult care is not affordable or available, children at home alone need preparation for their safety and security. During "off hours" concerned parents like Barbara are careful not to overburden their children with additional responsibilities: "Even though my oldest son seems to have developed a lot of responsibility from the experience, I don't want to put too much on him. I still want him to do the things kids do—the extracurricular things."

Your Security Check

The attitudes and emotions you have about leaving your child alone are fundamental to the success of your arrangement. Before you undertake self-care, you must first examine your own feelings about it. Your attitudes about self-care can be indirectly transmitted to children. Your fears, worries, and uncertainties can be sensed by youngsters, causing them to be upset, too. Guilt over leaving children alone or mistrust of your child can turn an otherwise workable arrangement into a nightmare. June Kirby, struggling with after-school arrangements for her eight-year-old daughter, told us why she refused to leave Nickey in self-care:

> She's too mature to be in a day care center. I took her out because there were no kids there her age, and she was being used to take care of the younger children. She's never stayed home alone by herself because she's too afraid. She's too young to stay by herself because she couldn't defend herself. She's so friendly she might let a stranger in the house. And if I set rules she probably wouldn't follow them.

The mother is insecure about Nickey's being alone and is smart to work out an alternative. Nickey agrees with her mother's view: "I'd like to go home, but I'm scared to stay there by myself because there's been a lot of kidnapping in my neighborhood." Insecure parents beget insecure home-alone children.

Your first step in deciding if home-alone arrangements are for you and your family is to examine your true feelings. The quiz in box 1–1 will help you do this.

Add the numbers that you put in the blanks. The total will give you your Self-Care Security Score. Possible scores range from ten (extremely secure) to forty (extremely insecure). The higher your score the more insecure you are about leaving your child home alone. The lower your score, the more secure you are about it. The following key will help you interpret your score.

Score

Ten to nineteen = You are *very secure* about leaving your child in self-care.

Twenty to twenty-nine = You are *moderately insecure* about leaving your child home alone.

Thirty to forty = You are *very insecure* about leaving your child in self-care.

Box 1–1   THE SELF-CARE SECURITY QUIZ

In the blank before each statement use one of the following numbers to indicate your truthful answer about your child: 1 = Almost never true; 2 = Seldom true; 3 = Often true; 4 = Almost always true.

_____ 1. I often feel *guilty* when I think about leaving my child in self-care.

_____ 2. I *fear* that my child is developing (or would develop) permanent emotional damage from being home alone for a few hours a day.

_____ 3. I am *embarrassed* that I must leave my child at home alone because of no other choices.

_____ 4. I constantly *worry* about my child's safety in my absence.

_____ 5. I am *confused* on the one hand with the advantages of my child's independence and on the other with worry for my child's safety.

_____ 6. I am *uncertain* that self-care is the best thing for my child.

_____ 7. I am *afraid* that my child may resent me for not being home more.

_____ 8. The thought of leaving my child home alone makes me feel *anxious.*

_____ 9. I tend to get (would tend to get) easily *irritated* trying to balance my work plus the concern over my child being home alone.

_____ 10. The *stress* of having a child come home to an empty house would (does) interfere with my work productivity.

TOTAL _____ SCORE	

It's only natural that you would be concerned with your underage child's staying at home alone. But extreme insecurity about self-care arrangements can put more stress on your family than you may be willing to bear. You may discover that the emotional expense is not worth the financial savings and that some of the alternatives to self-care that we will discuss later suit your needs better. As you look back over your answers to the questions, notice the names of the feelings in italic print. Circle the ones beside which you wrote a "three" or "four." That will tell you a lot about the emotions that self-care arrangements bring out in you. Barbara Jordan took this test and scored thirty-two. Her list of feelings included fear, guilt, worry, confusion, uncertainty, anxiety, and irritation. She was surprised just how insecure and stressful she felt leaving her boys home alone.

If you are very secure about self-care arrangements, read on. This book will help you provide additional supports to make you feel even more confident about your child's self-care arrangements. If you are very or moderately insecure about leaving your child home alone, you will discover how to establish a secure self-care arrangement that will be reassuring to both you and your child. Or you will learn of other care arrangements that better fit your situation.

Parents who are concerned enough to worry are concerned enough to provide the best for their children. This book can help ease your mind. With some forethought and planning, you can rid yourself of guilt, shame, and worry while providing the best arrangement humanly and financially possible.

2

What Should You Do before Deciding on Home-Alone Care for Your Child?

Once you have examined your personal feelings about self-care, the next step is to think about the effect the arrangement will have on your child. Children adjust differently to self-care, depending upon personal and situational characteristics. Although you may feel comfortable with the arrangement at first, you may decide, after a closer look, that your child's immaturity, bad neighborhood location, or other factors are not suitable for him or her to stay home alone.

Every self-care arrangement must be tailored to fit the multiple aspects of each child. Before diving headlong into self-care arrangements, there are eight things you should do:

- Examine your attitude.
- Consider your child's age.
- Observe your child's maturity level.
- Prepare your child for the basics of self-care.
- Examine the safety of your neighborhood.
- Check your community resources.
- Determine the length of time your child will be alone.
- Decide on some type of check system in your absence.

Examine Your Attitude

Your feelings about leaving your child alone are fundamental to the success of your arrangement. If you feel secure about the prospects of self-care for your child, chances are your son or daughter also will feel secure about being home alone. By the same token, your child's feelings will bear on your attitude. If your child is agreeable, at ease, or even excited, then you will have a more positive outlook. But a disagreeable, apprehensive, or angry child will cause you to react more negatively. Let your feelings guide whatever action you take.

The best way to examine your attitude is to know how your child feels. Emotional preparation for you and your child is the first major step. A climate of mutual trust and open communication is the key to successful adjustment to self-care. Emotional preparation frequently is overlooked. Talking openly with your child about his or her feelings about being alone helps you examine your own attitude and find out how your child feels about this big step. Your child may be afraid to be alone, but she may be willing to give it a try. On the other hand, he may be terrified of going home to an empty house in the afternoon and say so. Or he may be excited about the plan because it makes him feel grown-up. Never assume how your child feels. Keep an open and honest dialogue between the two of you before deciding on self-care. After self-care is under way, periodic conversations and evaluations will help you know where you stand.

Sometimes children have apprehensions they won't always admit to because they want to do their part when parents have to work. You can listen to what children say and ask and what they do not say and ask. Body language and abrupt behavior changes are tell-tale signs of any discomfort or anxiety. Sudden aggressive behaviors or abrupt withdrawal could indicate a child's frustration or anxiety. If your child starts biting her fingernails or fidgeting nervously during discussions about being alone, she could be telling you she is frightened. Encouraging her to talk about her fears and worries and helping her to resolve them gives you and her a more positive attitude about the experience. Allowing time for talk and showing you love and care about your child through generous time and patience builds positive attitudes on both sides. Time to talk with her mom was the thing twelve-year-old Ruchi missed most about home-alone routines:

Box 2–1. Deciding on Home-Alone Care

Before making your final decision on home-alone care for your child, you should ask yourself eight critical questions. A "no" to any of these questions indicates that your child could encounter adjustment problems and that home-alone arrangements should be reconsidered.

_____ 1. Do I have a positive attitude toward my child's home-alone experience?

_____ 2. Is my child old enough to be left alone?

_____ 3. Is my child emotionally mature enough, regardless of age, to assume the responsibility of self-care?

_____ 4. Has my child been adequately prepared for the basics of self-care?

_____ 5. Does my family live in a safe neighborhood where crime is low and community cohesion high?

_____ 6. Can neighbors and community facilities be depended upon as support systems?

_____ 7. Will my child be in self-care for short time periods?

_____ 8. Will my child have some type of distant or close adult supervision during self-care?

If parents have to work, they should be around their kids a lot when they get home and talk to them. The kids across the street get to see their mom all the time and I'm jealous because they get to go off and their parents are always there for them. Sometimes Mom's not there for me. If she'd be here more, I could talk to her a lot better, and I could talk about my problems to her. But it's hard to talk to my mom because she works so much. When I have a problem, I usually talk to my sister because she understands better.

Consider Your Child's Age

There is no magic age at which children can begin staying home alone. By nature, self-care has certain characteristics, such as self-sufficiency and decision making, that require children to adjust to premature responsibilities. Because of these inherent characteristics, a good rule of thumb is to assume that most children younger than age eleven are too young for the responsibilities of self-care. A nine-year-old boy who stays by himself every day said, "I'm scared when the wall cracks. I lock the door and hide when I'm scared." Some extremely young children are placed in situations that can be categorized as child neglect. Take five-year-old Luke, for example. In the large city where he lives, Luke gets off his school bus and patiently waits on his doorstep for two hours until his mother gets home from work. The child has just started kindergarten, which is a big step in itself. But having to wait without adult supervision for such a long time imposes even more stress and burden on Luke that children his age are not old enough to handle.

Responsible adults must play matchmaker between an age of protection and an age of preparation to nurture children through self-care situations. Most parents and some experts use the ages of eleven and twelve as a benchmark for self-care status. In our survey of 886 parents, we found that children between the ages of nine and eleven (53 percent) were left alone more often than children between the ages of five and eight (13 percent) or between the ages of twelve and fourteen (34 percent). Self-care increases with grade level and reaches a peak during sixth grade (at approximately age eleven or twelve) when parent care drops drastically and continues to decline through the ninth grade (see figure 2–1). Statistics from a U.S. Census of sixty thousand households show that one-half of the children in self-care are ten years old or older.

Although a benchmark age can never be the single factor in deciding on self-care arrangements, the age span of eleven to twelve does hold some merit. Among many cultures of the world, this is a time when children become caretakers of younger siblings while parents work. In India and other parts of Asia, Mexico, Africa, and North America, children have reached "the age of reason" by eleven or twelve and are expected to care for themselves to some degree as well as supervise younger brothers and sisters. Twelve-year-old Nyansango girls from Kenya, for example, are put in charge of their baby brothers and sisters until the children can walk alone. They must feed, bathe, and watch over themselves as well as their siblings while their mothers work in nearby gardens or go to the market.

This age range is also a natural transition time when children mature mentally and begin to think in more adult-like terms (even though they still do not have the same mental abilities as adults). This new way of

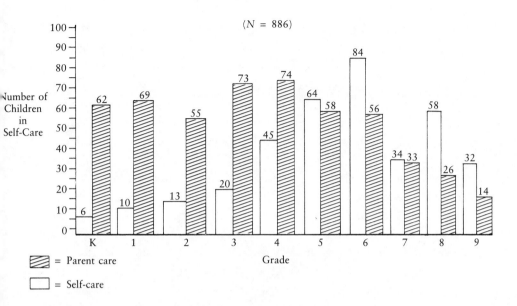

Figure 2–1. FREQUENCY OF CHILDREN IN SELF-CARE VERSUS
PARENT-CARE ARRANGEMENTS, BY GRADE

thinking is partly biological and partly learned. It allows children to handle more responsibility and unexpected situations and to make sounder decisions about their welfare and safety. It becomes easier for them to judge whom to talk to and whom not to talk to on the way home from school, how to answer the telephone and door appropriately when a stranger calls, how to handle emergencies, how to supervise younger children, and how to prepare nutritional foods.

You may be thinking, "But what about my eight-year-old? I cannot afford after-school care. Home-alone care is my only choice." Although we advise the ideal ages of eleven or twelve for beginning home-alone care, we meet many parents who raise these questions. And we know that there are thousands of six-, seven-, and eight-year olds at home alone because their parents have no other options. If you're in the same boat, you must remember that age is only one factor among many that should be considered. The child's maturity level is an overriding factor that always outweighs age.

Observe Your Child's Maturity Level

It is a mistake to assume that all eleven- and twelve-year-olds are candidates for self-care. There is a wide range of social and emotional maturation rates that differ for each child. Some children are still not mature enough to take care of themselves by age fourteen or fifteen. Others may be ready by eight or nine years. Developmentally, younger children lack the necessary mental and emotional skills for sensible decision making. They cannot foresee all possibilities and problems that can arise when they break the agreed-upon rules and regulations. Too many tragedies have been reported when very young children are left alone for only a brief time. Even when they have committed rules to memory, the impulse of the moment takes over their actions and clouds their judgment. The child-like side dominates, and all the rehearsed safety plans are forgotten. One nine-year-old boy entrusted all responsibilities to his fourteen-year-old sister: ''I don't answer the telephone. My sister is supposed to do that. If it rings before she gets there, I just let it ring. If the doorbell rings, we just turn off the TV and stay still.'' Older children, like this fourteen-year-old sister, take on supervisory obligations with greater ease but still need adult direction and guidance.

Maturity for self-care is a gradual process that begins long before the school-age years. The journey starts when toddlers begin to exercise their independence within the boundaries of a parental safety net. The toddler takes that first step and reaches for curious objects to explore. There are gentle ''no-no's,'' and breakable objects are put out of reach on high shelves. Under the parent's close guidance, children learn such self-care responsibilities as putting on sweaters, fastening shoes, and staying out of the street. Errors and mistakes occur within a parental safety buffer where no threats exist to body or mind.

In those earliest days, parents are solely responsible for their child's safety. Consider two-year-old Kevin, who refuses to let his father hold his hand as they walk through the shopping mall. And Alisha, a three-year-old who comes bounding into the room, stomping with her new cowgirl boots, refusing to take them off even for a nap. Gradually, parents relinquish control to the child and act as a guide to wise decision making. Limited choices are given: whether to have a second helping of peas, to play with blocks or to paint, or to stay with Daddy or go with Mommy to the supermarket. These simple decisions keep the shield of protection in place yet promote autonomy—the bedrock for later self-care responsibilities.

When children reach age eleven or twelve, they have many more opportunities to practice self-reliance. They are away from their families for longer periods of time and can venture into unknown waters. The teacher, scout leader, or other community leader provides guideposts by calling a halt to unacceptable behaviors. With experience, school-age children learn their limits and can follow rules and regulations. Still, seven-year-olds are developmentally different from fourteen-year-olds. Maturity differences explain why some younger children are more afraid than others and why six thousand children a year die in accidents and fires at home alone. Teenagers can usually handle greater responsibility for their safety and welfare than nine-year-olds because they are more mature emotionally and mentally. Younger children need closer adult supervision before and after school, while upper elementary and junior high school children still need supervision but can handle more on their own. So the type of supervision must be tailored to the child's level of maturity.

Growing evidence suggests that parents self-select which children stay home alone, based on signs of their child's independence and maturity. A U.S. Census of sixty thousand households found that parents make the decision of self-care as a choice, not out of necessity. Parents choose self-care after they judge their children to be mature and independent enough to be home alone. But, you may ask, how do I know if my child has reached this stage of responsibility?

Certain clues will tell you if your child is mature enough to stay home alone. Ask yourself the following questions. Does your child:

- Follow rules and exercise self-control in your presence?
- Think logically and show the ability to problem-solve?
- Set goals and work toward them?
- Handle brief periods alone when you run out to do an errand?
- Occupy himself or herself during free time without getting bored easily or feeling lonely?
- Follow through with commitments or daily household chores?
- Remember and keep his or her side of the bargain when you have an agreement about something?

- Show respect for another person's property?
- Demonstrate the ability to judge right from wrong?
- Read, write, and talk well enough to recall events and explain situations that you experience together?
- Exhibit signs of being overly fearful even in your presence?
- Face unexpected situations with calm and flexibility, instead of alarm and hysteria?
- Demonstrate good physical coordination to maneuver in and out of situations around the house while avoiding clumsiness and physical injury?

Your child's maturity is an important component in planning safe home-alone care. Use the scale in box 2–2 to rate your child's maturity level.

You can usually pick up hints from casual observation to determine when or if your child has reached a satisfactory maturity level. Some children give direct messages that eliminate any second-guessing about self-care readiness. A six-year-old boy said, "I don't like going home by myself. I wish somebody was there. I don't like for my mother to work. She calls me at home from work to check on me. But I'm still afraid when somebody knocks at the door. I just don't answer it, and I don't answer the telephone either. I just let it ring." Chronologically and emotionally unprepared, this child limps through his days alone after school.

Even at twelve years old, some children are too afraid, too bored, or too lonely by themselves. Lauren, for example, started showing signs of immaturity after her home-alone arrangement was under way:

Sometimes I'm afraid people are watching me and know when I'm alone. Once a green Volkswagen sat at the end of my driveway for a long time. When my mom came down the street, it left. I used to worry about losing my house key, and I'd leave it at school a lot. But now we put it in a certain place, and I have to worry about someone hiding in a closet. I get scared easily. It's boring by myself. I just do my homework. I don't watch TV. I asked Mom if I could go to a day care because I'm tired of being alone. There is nobody to talk to.

Box 2–2   Your Child's Maturity Level
Rate your child using the scale from 1 to 4 on each of the twelve items below. 1 = Strongly disagree; 2 = Disagree; 3 = Agree; 4 = Strongly agree.

_____ 1. My child has a history of responsible behavior.

_____ 2. My child is argumentative.

_____ 3. My child follows rules and has self-control in my presence.

_____ 4. My child has trouble keeping promises and following rules.

_____ 5. My child has a history of using good judgment.

_____ 6. My child gets scared at nightfall even when I'm at home.

_____ 7. My child is content to entertain him or herself.

_____ 8. My child prefers that others entertain him or her.

_____ 9. My child follows directions well.

_____ 10. My child gets upset when something unexpected happens.

_____ 11. My child shows respect for other people's property.

_____ 12. My child is clumsy and poorly coordinated.

TOTAL _____ **SCORE**	Total the scores for all the *odd* items and enter your total in the space to the left.

A child who is argumentative, has trouble keeping promises, depends on others for amusement, is easily scared and upset, and poorly coordinated is generally more immature than the child who is responsible, follows rules, uses good judgment, entertains self, follows directions well, and shows respect for other people's property. While the above scale is not standardized, it does provide a general picture of whether your child is mature enough for self-care. Mature behaviors are associated with the *odd* items. The higher the *odd* total, the more mature your child is likely to behave when home alone. In contrast, the higher the *even* total, the less mature your child is likely to behave at home alone.

Heather, an older and more mature twelve-year-old, comes home from school, unlocks her front door, and secures it behind her. She calls her mother at work to tell her she is home safe and sound and spends the next two hours doing homework until her mom gets home. Heather has strict rules that she must follow. She knows she is not to allow strangers or friends inside when her mother is working. Heather has a routine she follows every afternoon and feels secure about that. Being home alone for a few hours a day makes her feel self-reliant and responsible.

Prepare Your Child for the Basics of Self-Care

Aside from this early developmental start, you must give your child adequate instruction and preparation *before* you place him or her in self-care. Some parents set themselves up for failure by leaving their children alone first and then starting preparation after the arrangements are well under way. You wouldn't wait until you go to the hospital to have a baby to take prepared childbirth classes. The thought of it sounds silly. Preparation means ''before'' and that's when it should come, not during. Beginning self-care and then trying to prepare your child can turn an otherwise positive experience into a nightmare.

A quick-fix approach to home-alone care will not work either. Adequate preparation takes time. Commit yourself to taking the time to prepare your child with rules, routines, developing a contract together, and practicing what to do in an emergency or accident. A few minutes or a few rules thrown at a child is a quick fix that will not replace proper preparation: ''Richard, I want you to come straight home, lock the door, and don't let anyone in until I get home.'' If you are willing to put the time into preparing your child for self-care, the rewards will pay off once you have launched the arrangement. But if you take the quick-fix approach, eventually your child and you will pay the price.

You should set limits and point out dangerous pitfalls of carelessness and poor judgment. Providing children's books on safety and self-care skills for your child will strengthen his or her confidence. Be sure to pay attention to the physical environment by providing securely locked doors and windows. The importance of home security to the child's psychological well-being was reflected in an eleven-year-old boy's comment: ''I'm afraid that somebody may be in the house on the days the side door doesn't latch good.'' The next chapter will tell you all the home-alone skills you will need to learn with your child.

There are other, more official, ways that you can prepare your family for self-care. Numerous training programs have been developed to prepare unsupervised children to handle more responsibility while parents work. Girl Scouts of America has published a survival skills booklet called *Safe and Sound at Home Alone;* Boy Scouts of America puts out a manual called *Prepared for Today;* Camp Fire, Inc. produced a program titled *I Can Do It* for children between second and fourth grades. One of the best programs available for parents and their home-alone children is called *I'm in Charge.* This is a course to help parents and children between fourth and eighth grades learn about self-care. Parents learn of the risks of self-care and how to reduce them. Children learn personal safety skills, how to respond in emergencies, and how to identify and deal with problems. Feelings about being home alone are explored together by parents and children. The final session brings parents and children together to develop contracts for their own agreed-upon self-care arrangements. Check chapter 7 for where to write for more information and for other resources that will help you bolster your child's self-care arrangements.

Examine the Safety of Your Neighborhood

You must examine the safety of your own neighborhood in terms of physical and psychological risks to your child. The places where self-care children live can make a difference in whether they are vulnerable to physical or psychological harm. City children living in high-crime areas are at greater risk than those who live in relatively safe, crime-free settings in rural or suburban areas. City children usually are more confined and isolated and face greater threats of personal intrusion and accidents. In contrast, children in nonurban neighborhoods have fewer threats of personal harm from outside sources. Rural and suburban home-alone children and those in adult supervision after school benefit more than city youngsters in every way. They are superior in academic achievement, self-reliance, and self-concept. They have fewer fears, experience less boredom and loneliness, and are less vulnerable to accidents. Their play is less restricted and they have fewer social and emotional problems.

Parents of urban children may need to set closer supervision and tighter rules than those of children in small towns or rural areas. Ten-year-old Lauren is younger than the eleven- to twelve-year-old cut-off point. Although her young age, combined with living in a large city, makes her uneasy about being home alone, she has the benefits of nearby neighbors who watch out for her:

> I live in the city. I get home at three-thirty, and my mom doesn't get home until five-thirty. Once I went home, and my dad was there, but I didn't know it because the door was locked. I un-locked it, and the TV was on. I checked the bedrooms, but I didn't see anybody. I heard noises too. I was scared so I went outside and waited fifteen minutes. Then I looked in the window and saw my dad. I get my key from the same place every day, and I'm afraid somebody is watching me, but it doesn't bother me now as much as it used to. I can use the microwave but not the stove. I've learned to not use the stove to cook because I might start a grease fire. I don't really know how to put out a grease fire—I just know to put salt on it. I know not to mess with the guns or knives. I don't search every room each day. My mom said if I heard some-thing, just run outside and to the neighbors. They keep an eye on me. I just fix a sandwich, a cookie, and a Pepsi. I saw the movie *Adam*. He had to come home alone. I've learned not to talk to strangers and to get out of the house if there is trouble.

Children who live in fairly safe neighborhoods in suburban or rural areas tend to do better when home alone. A thirteen-year-old girl who lives in a rural neighborhood said: "I enjoy being alone because I have time to think, and it gives me a sense of responsibility. There are four houses within walking distance of mine, and I can always contact my grandparents who live down the road."

Those in high-crime areas where neighborhood solidarity is low have more problems. A less fortunate eleven-year-old-boy reported low com-munity cohesion: "I live in a two-story white frame house, and I live around a lot of old people, and old people can't help you if something happens. So it's kind of scary. They'd say, 'I can't right now' or 'We don't want to get involved with it.' So you just have to protect yourself on your own." Parents who judge their neighborhoods as too unsafe with few support systems may be putting their children in physical and psychological jeopardy.

Check Your Community Resources

Many children at home alone feel secure because of nearby neighbors whom they could contact for help. Some children routinely check in with a neighbor after school, and others entrust door keys to neighbors in case they misplace theirs. Children who know their neighbors and know they can depend on them feel more comfortable being alone. An eleven-year-old boy said, "I've never been scared alone. I have neighbors nearby, and if I had to, I could go and get them to help out."

One day after school, five-year-old Jamie jumped off some steps into a broken plastic crate, severely cutting his leg and requiring twenty-five stitches. His mother was working, and his sitter, a sixth-grade neighborhood girl, did not know where Jamie's mother worked. There was no telephone in the house. The mother had hired the sixth grader because she could not afford after-school care. Dangers in this situation are related to lack of proper supervision for the child. Generally speaking, sixth-grade children are barely old and mature enough to supervise themselves, much less younger children. The second mistake that reduced Jamie's adult contact was the lack of a telephone—his lifeline to his mother, neighbors, and community emergency services. Neither the children nor the parent was familiar with local community facilities that could add some safety features to this risky self-care arrangement. Improper preparation for emergencies complicated Jamie's accident and left the sixth-grade girl, Jamie, and his mother in an emotional aftermath. The mother felt terribly guilty about the accident and finally found an adult sitter to stay with Jamie after school.

Community facilities play an essential role in self-care arrangements. Emergency services (such as police, fire, and rescue departments) should be within reasonable distance and their telephone numbers readily available so that your child feels an extra anchor of security. Your child should know where a telephone is available if not at your house and should know when and how to get help if there is an emergency. A fourteen-year-old girl felt confident with her emergency plan: "I've never had an emergency, but if I had to call the police or fire department, I have their numbers.''

Determine the Length of Time Your Child Will Be Alone

Time alone can be a major factor in children's adjustment. Children who spend unusually long hours in self-care are more likely to have more adjustment problems. The longer they are alone, the greater are their chances of having an accident or expressing fears, especially after nightfall. Steve's mother and stepfather work irregular hours, and they do not always have the same hours. They may arrive home at five, six, or nine at night. Steve calls his mother to find out when someone will be there. Steve's uncertainty and anxiety over his parents' irregular work schedules cause him to be anxious during school hours, says his teacher. Throughout the school day, the eight-year-old never knows how long he will be alone when he gets home each afternoon. Steve doesn't need a key to his empty house because the door lock is broken. But once inside, he can lock the door from within. He calls his mother first thing. Then he watches television. He is very protective of his dog, Brownie, and worries that other animals in the neighborhood will eat his dog's food. One child, an older girl, has permission to visit Steve, although she doesn't come over often. Asked about how he felt staying home alone, he replied, ''Sometimes lonely, sometimes scared.'' Steve's biggest fears are Brownie's barking and noises. He hides in the bathroom when he gets scared and says, ''If I think somebody is trying to get in, I get a knife.'' At five o'clock, if no one is home, Steve walks across the street to the day care to pick up his three-year-old sister, Stacy.

There are many problems with this self-care arrangement. His young age, inadequate preparation, lack of supervision, and added burden of a three-year-old sister place him in additional jeopardy. Steve is too young to have been left alone. No eight-year-old child should have to resort to hiding in the bathroom with a knife. Despite his young age, proper thought and planning could relieve Steve of much anxiety. Repairing the door lock would add an element of security for him as he enters the house each afternoon. If Steve absolutely has to stay alone, he needs the security of knowing the exact number of hours he will be home by himself and those hours should be short and consistent from one day to the next. Steve's parents should make other arrangements for the supervision of their three-year-old daughter when her day care center closes. Eight-year-olds have their hands full taking care of themselves without a small child to watch. Smart parents, having considered all these risk factors, would never have started this child in self-care.

Longer hours also are more likely to produce boredom and loneliness. Brian, an eleven-year-old who is alone for eight hours until eleven-thirty every night, said, "In the afternoons it's boring and lonely, and at night it's scary." Shorter time periods work best. One or two hours is enough time for children to complete homework and chores and to enjoy some time alone. Jennifer, an eight-year-old, is alone for one hour in the afternoons and says she likes it: "I'm usually not scared. It makes me feel big." Jennifer's one hour in the afternoon is a dramatic contrast to Brian's eight hours at night and shows how amount of time alone can affect children's adjustment. You will need to think through the length of time your child will be alone. If your child is very young and the time will be more than two hours, you should look elsewhere for care arrangements.

Decide on Some Type of Check System in Your Absence

The degree to which your child has some kind of adult contact in your absence will make a difference in his or her adjustment. There are different levels of supervision that can be provided, depending upon your own unique work and home situation. Parents almost always have some control over how much supervision their children have before and after school. If you cannot be there, you can call or have a child check with you, another adult, or older brother or sister. Or you can have firm rules to temporarily replace your immediate authority. Under no circumstances should children be allowed to roam their neighborhoods unsupervised after school.

Some parents may have a neighbor closely supervise their children. David, a fourth grader, goes directly to a neighbor's house to check in before he goes home. If he needs anything, he contacts the neighbor, who keeps a watchful eye on him. He can play outdoors, visit with his friends, and have a snack that was left for him that morning. Other parents supervise their children by calling them from work or by having their children call them as soon as they get home from school. Daily telephone calls from his mother provide a lifeline for one seven-year-old boy: "I like going home by myself. I play in my room. I like for my mom to work. I call her sometimes, and sometimes she calls me. I'm never afraid of things." When telephone calls are not possible, agreed-upon rules act as *in absentia* guidelines to undergird afternoons with a sense of comfort and security for both parents and children.

Some parents have an older child who can assume supervisory responsibilities. Sibling care arrangements, although sometimes workable, also can cause problems. The older child may resent the added responsibility, or constant squabbling between siblings can complicate an already stressful situation, as this eight-year-old girl reports: "My brother (fourteen years old) beats me up and plays tricks on me. One time he folded me up in the sofa bed, and another time he went off and left me by myself."

On the other hand, twelve-year-old Ruchi enjoys having her older sister at home to confide in:

Since Mom's not here all the time, I talk to my sister more, and me and my sister are real close. We get along real good, and I think that's why. Things are not always so great, though. Sometimes my sister is home, but she's not really with you because she's mad at something and she's yelling at you for no reason and my mom's not there to do anything about it.

Barbara Jordan says that when summertime comes and the kids are out of school, her older son is sick and tired of watching his younger brother: "My older son is ready for summer vacation, and he gets mad at his brother because he has to babysit. But since I have to work and cannot afford day care, there's no other choice. That's just the way it has to be." As you can see, although sibling supervision is not ideal, sometimes it is the best arrangement that some parents can make.

Twelve-year-old Patti does not go directly home after school. She stops off at the park, goes by the shopping mall, and sometimes visits at a friend's house. Because Patti has no set routine, no direct adult supervision, and no predictable setting in the afternoon, her personal safety is jeopardized. Situations in which unsupervised children float freely in their neighborhoods or at the local video arcade often lead to poor adjustment and such negative consequences as accidents, abductions, and crime.

Before deciding on self-care, think about some type of check-in system for your child in your absence. Make sure you have answered the following questions to your satisfaction:

- Will my child promptly report home after school and telephone me right away or check in with a reliable neighbor?
- Will my child stop off at a friend's house where there is no adult supervison?
- Will my child frequent a favorite "hang-out"?
- Will I establish rules for my child to follow inside and outside the home in my absence?

Will Your Child Be at Risk? Take **HART**

The **HART** quiz in box 2–3 can help you measure the risk that self-care holds for your child. **HART** stands for Home-Alone Risk Test. It lists the eight chief components important for home-alone care. When combined, the eight items can add up to put some children in self-care at risk. But in the right combination, they give rise to successful home-alone care for children. Read each characteristic and decide how well it pertains to your child. Using the scale from one to five, rate your own particular situation by circling the number that best describes the home-alone care you have or plan to have.

Once you have rated your child in each category, you are ready to compute your child's **HART** score. Add the eight numbers that you circled under each category: **HART = YOUR ATTITUDE + CHILD'S AGE + CHILD'S MATURITY LEVEL + DEGREE OF PREPARATION + LOCATION + COMMUNITY RESOURCES + AMOUNT OF TIME LEFT ALONE + TYPE OF CHECK SYSTEM IN YOUR ABSENCE.**

Box 2-3 YOUR CHILD'S HART SCORE

1. Your Attitude

| 1 Extremely secure | 2 Secure | 3 In between | 4 Insecure | 5 Extremely insecure |

2. Child's Age

| 1 Fourteen and over | 2 Twelve to thirteen | 3 Ten to eleven | 4 Seven to nine | 5 Six and under |

3. Child's Maturity Level

| 1 Extremely mature | 2 Mature | 3 In between | 4 Immature | 5 Extremely immature |

4. Degree of Preparation

| 1 Very well prepared | 2 Well prepared | 3 Quick fix | 4 Unprepared | 5 Extremely unprepared |

5. Location That Best Describes Where You Live

| 1 Rural area | 2 Suburbia | 3 Small town | 4 City (pop. under 300,000) | 5 City (pop. over 300,000) |

6. Community Resources

| 1 Excellent | 2 Good | 3 Average | 4 Fair | 5 Poor |

7. Daily Length of Time Left Alone

| 1 One hour | 2 Two hours | 3 Three hours | 4 Four hours | 5 Five hours or more |

8. Type of Check System in Your Absence

| 1 Closely supervised by neighbor or other adult | 2 Supervised by parent *in absentia* (daily phone calls and clear set of rules) | 3 Supervised at home by older sibling | 4 Unsupervised at friend's house | 5 Unsupervised, hanging out in neighborhood |

Score Sheet

_____ 1. Your attitude

_____ 2. Child's age

_____ 3. Child's maturity level

_____ 4. Degree of preparation

_____ 5. Location of neighborhood

_____ 6. Community resources

_____ 7. Daily length of time left alone

_____ 8. Type of check system in your absence

_____ **TOTAL SCORE**

Understanding Your Child's **HART** Score

The higher your score, the higher the risk to your child when left alone. A score from eight to twenty is a low-risk score. Low-risk children are those who have few or none of the combinations that would cause them to be hurt from being alone. Twelve-year-old Marie, for example, lives in a Lincolnton, N.C., suburb, where she spends her one hour alone after school doing homework, after calling her mom to let her know she's home. Her rules are to do her chores, keep the house in order, complete homework before watching television, and not turn on the oven. Marie is well-prepared for her self-care and says she enjoys staying home alone and is seldom afraid.

A score from twenty-one to thirty is a moderate-risk score. Moderate-risk children are those who have some, but not all, combinations to place them at risk. A good example is fourteen-year-old Sam, who lives in Washington, D.C., and is alone for five hours every afternoon, but who calls his mother as soon as he gets home and has clear rules about what he can and cannot do. Sam's maturity and preparation for self-care offset his parents' extreme insecurities about leaving him alone.

A score of thirty-one to forty is a high-risk score that contains many or all of the ingredients that place children at risk in self-care. Typically, high-risk children are the extreme exceptions. John, a mature six-year-old, lives in Philadelphia and comes home each day to an empty house.

John's mother reluctantly took a new job without preparing her child to be alone. She is plagued by guilt and worried about leaving her young child alone but needs the money. John's mother works odd hours, which requires that he care for himself between three and eight P.M. Because she doesn't know her neighbors well and doesn't have a telephone, his mother cannot check on him as she would like to. So, instead of staying home, he usually hangs out at a local video arcade. John has the highest possible risk score of all three children.

This simple test is intended only as a thumbnail sketch and pause for thought about self-care situations. Still, a higher score could indicate greater risks of having accidents, getting into trouble, and being exposed to sexual victimization. It is possible, too, that higher-risk children could face educational and social obstacles, such as low academic achievement and poor self-esteem and social adjustment than lower-risk children. You can use information from the **HART** to help reduce any risk your self-care situation could bring before your child ever begins. If your child has a moderate- or high-risk score, take heart. Think about how you can improve your child's situation. Take steps to reduce the risk that you have identified or make other suitable arrangements.

Workable Self-Care Arrangements

By definition, workable self-care arrangements must match the unique needs of each child and family. As you have seen, you can examine your own arrangements to determine your child's adjustment through eight **HART** ingredients. Each of these ingredients combines in unique ways to contribute to children's different levels of adjustment. Many home-alone children are doing well and growing and developing in healthy ways. They are the ones whose parents have "taken to heart" all eight **HART** components. Ultimately, checks and balances between protection and preparation lay in the hands of parents. We will present a more detailed discussion of suggestions for parents in the next chapter. Meanwhile, words from a wise single mother with two children in self-care speak to all other parents planning self-care arrangements:

I think, typically, we feel a lot of stress, and I think we are frustrated by lots of things. And I think it's important that we are very careful that we don't take our frustrations out on our children—that we make them feel as comfortable as we can—that they know they can call Mom or Dad, maybe, if they feel unsafe for some reason. Or it's important that there's somebody in the neighborhood that knows that they [the children] are alone, and they can go to that particular person until Mom can get home to handle the situation. I also think it's important that you listen to your kids. It's important that you listen anyway, but somehow or another it becomes even more important to me that I actually hear what they're saying. So I try very hard to listen and sometimes it's kind of hard between the kids, the job, and the home. It's hard making all the decisions, and sometimes I wonder if I'll ever get a chance to take care of me. But there's no ''ifs,'' ''ands,'' or ''buts'' about it—I have to do it!

3

How Can You Plan the Best
Home-Alone Care?

N OTHING is more terrifying to home-alone children than losing a
house key. Pale and out of breath, a ten-year-old child rushed into
the school office recently. Voice shaking, he nervously asked the question that the school secretary hears a dozen times a day. "Have you seen
my key? It has a blue plastic tag on it."

When the secretary, smile on her face, retrieved the key and handed
it to the youngster, he breathed such a huge sigh of relief the papers
flopped on her desk.

A principal at an elementary school in Charlotte, N.C., constantly
finds in the hallways, gym, cafeteria, and classrooms house keys that slip
out of the pockets of elementary school youngsters. "I'm amazed at
how many young children are given the responsibility of taking care of
themselves in mornings and afternoons while parents work," she said.
"But most of the parents must work and have no other choice but to
leave children on their own."

At some point, you may be one of these parents. You have made your
decision about self-care and are now ready to begin preparing your child
to be home alone. Preventing your house key from ending up in the
school office is just one of the many steps you can take in your preparation plans as your child begins staying home alone.

Often it is difficult for parents to decide the best plan for home-alone
kids. School-age children are not all alike, and neither are the
neighborhoods in which they live. Different needs from child to child
and community to community have resulted in multiple programs to

match the development needs of youngsters and their families. Keep in mind that an eight-year-old has different needs and interests from a fourteen-year-old. As such, younger children need closer out-of-school supervision, while upper elementary and junior high students still need supervision, in which they know adults are available, but can be allowed more self-reliance. Still, regardless of age, parents should address certain common points for all children as they begin to prepare and practice a safe home-alone plan. You should examine the safety of your home and neighborhood in terms of physical and psychological risks. Where such risks prevail, you can take proper safety steps to ensure your child's protection.

Sizing Up Your Neighborhood Resources

Begin by taking stock in your neighborhood. Does it have a low or high crime rate? What are the most common types of crime that occur in the neighborhood? The police department can supply this information. How heavily traveled are the roads surrounding your home? During what hours is traffic heaviest? Your local planning office can give you this information.

How close is your home to hospitals, police and fire stations, and emergency and poison control centers? Identify the locations of these service agencies on a simple map that you and your child develop together. Post the map on the refrigerator door, in your child's bedroom, or in some other special place.

Periodically check your child's ability to use the map by playing a game. Ask your child to use the map and direct a walk to each service agency within walking distance, or if too far to walk, drive to the agency while your child traces the route on the map. Upon arriving, chat with workers at the agency so that your child and the workers associate faces with names. Your child will feel more comfortable calling upon service agencies if a friendly relationship is established.

Crime rates, traffic flow, and location of service agencies are not the only neighborhood characteristics to consider. Next-door neighbors, the location of bus stops, and the characteristics of adjoining neighborhoods are some other factors to consider in sizing up the safety and danger areas. A more complete safety checklist for assessing a neighborhood is provided in box 3–1. This information will be used later to figure your safety buffer.

Box 3–1   NEIGHBORHOOD SAFETY CHECKLIST

Evaluate the areas of your neighborhood that are safe using the following checklist.

- ☐ Crime rate is low.
- ☐ Supervision is supplied by a well-trained and responsible adult.
- ☐ Traffic flow is light.
- ☐ Area is protected from traffic.
- ☐ At least one community agency that can respond to an emergency is located close by.
- ☐ Area is free of dangerous objects and equipment.
- ☐ Area is free of pollution.
- ☐ Area is protected from surrounding dangerous neighborhoods.
- ☐ Area allows for quiet activities.
- ☐ Police or security guards regularly patrol area.
- ☐ At least one adult leader is available for every ten children.
- ☐ A check-in system is used to document a child's presence.
- ☐ Activities are well supervised and developmentally appropriate.

[List other safety items you think are important.]

_____

_____

Considering all the safety items, check the areas of your neighborhood that are safe.

Area	Time of Safety	Name of Adult Supervision	Distance Home
☐ Park	_____	_____	_____
☐ Lake or pond	_____	_____	_____
☐ Recreation center	_____	_____	_____
☐ Shopping mall	_____	_____	_____
☐ Church	_____	_____	_____
☐ Library	_____	_____	_____
☐ School	_____	_____	_____
☐ Friend's home	_____	_____	_____
☐ Other	_____	_____	_____
_____	_____	_____	_____

Sizing Up the Physical Safety of Your Home

Your home represents a chief source of potential danger to your child when left alone. Consider the safety of utilities, unprotected electrical outlets, and unlabeled foods and medicines. Use the checklist in box 3–2 to evaluate the physical safety of your home.

Box 3–2   HOME SAFETY CHECKLIST

Are the following areas of your home safe?

YES	NO	
☐	☐	Electrical and mechanical equipment are locked away.
☐	☐	Locks are secure on all doors and windows.
☐	☐	A smoke alarm system is installed and operative.
☐	☐	Foods and medicines are separated and clearly labeled.
☐	☐	All appliances are in good working condition.
☐	☐	Directions for using appliances are clearly written and posted.
☐	☐	Electrical outlets are covered with a protective plate.
☐	☐	Broken electrical cords are replaced.
☐	☐	A map of local emergency service agencies is posted.
☐	☐	Emergency telephone numbers and names are posted.
☐	☐	A schedule of after-school activities is posted.
☐	☐	A list of safety dos and don'ts are posted.
☐	☐	Broken glass is replaced.
☐	☐	Areas where children may get trapped are secure.
☐	☐	Areas from or over which children may fall are secure.
☐	☐	The temperature of the home is self-regulated and comfortable.
☐	☐	Loud noises from surrounding area are masked.
☐	☐	Broken furniture is repaired or thrown away.
☐	☐	A check-in system is established.
☐	☐	Procedures are established for answering the telephone and door.

List those areas to which you responded with a NO.

Now list the steps you will take to change your no responses to yes responses.

The physical characteristics of your home represent only part of the safety prevention. Safety is also dependent upon your child's behavior. A broken appliance is safe if your child follows instructions not to use it. A wood-burning stove is safe if your child follows correct operating instructions and knows what to do in an accident. Clearly your child's competence is an important in-home safety feature. In general, older children are less at risk than younger ones. Responsible home-alone children are less at risk than irresponsible children. Other age and behavioral characteristics will help you determine your child's safety features:

Age	*Safety*
Five or younger	Very unsafe
Six to twelve	Somewhat safe
Thirteen or older	Most safe

Less Risky Behavior	*More Risky Behavior*
Responsible	Impulsive

Less Risky Behavior	*More Risky Behavior*
Introspective	Curious
Honest	Dishonest
Prefers indoor activities	Prefers outdoor activities
Good-natured	Argumentative
Good family relations	Poor family relations

Safety Buffer

The checklist from box 3–1 will help you establish a safety buffer surrounding your home. Follow these three steps:

1. **Location:** Are there areas surrounding your home that are safe during at least some part of the day?

    ☐ Yes   List the areas and how near they are to your home. Then go to step two.

    _____

    _____

    ☐ No   Stop. Your child's safety outside your home is not possible.

2. **Time:** Do the times of safety for each area meet your child's after-school needs?

    ☐ Yes   List the times of safety for each area. Then go to step three.

    _____

    _____

    ☐ No   Stop. Your child's safety outside your home is not possible.

3. **Adult contact:** Is at least one responsible adult available to check on your child's activities in each area?

☐ Yes   Name the adults for each area below.

_____

_____

☐ No   Stop. Your child's safety outside your home is
           questionable.

If your answers to the questions are all "yes," then your safety buffer
tells you *where, when,* and *with whom* your child's safety is assured. A
map that shows this information will provide a fuller picture of how to
implement the safety buffer. In some cases, location, time, and adult
contact buffers are present but not coordinated. The identified safety
areas within a neighborhood, for instance, may be accessible only by car
or with an adult escort. You can coordinate your safety time slot and
adult to get your child to and from these places. If coordination is not
possible, you will need to re-evaluate the practical use of your safety buffer. All three buffers must be in place for a home-alone child to be safe
outside the home.

If you answered "no" to items 1, 2, or 3, you have a limited safety
buffer. A safe space, time, and adult are needed to ensure your child's
well-being. But things can change. You need to recheck your safety buffer yearly. Our society is highly mobile and undergoing rapid change.
The characteristics of your neighborhood and home could change
drastically a year from now.

In-Home Safety Precautions

In addition to the physical safety of your neighborhood and home, you
must also have certain in-home strategies. Your plan should include
precautions with house keys, getting home, checking in, telephone
skills, house rules, and emergencies.

House Keys

The symbol most associated with home-alone kids is the house key.
Make sure your child learns the importance of keeping the key in a safe

---

Box 3–3   TEN STEPS TO SAFER HOME-ALONE CARE

While a latchkey home can never be judged as safe as one in which a child is supervised by a responsible adult, parents can provide a safer environment by following these tips.

1. **Keys.** Instruct your child to keep his or her house keys hidden inside a pocket, purse or wallet.

2. **Schedule.** Establish a daily schedule so that your child knows what to do when at home alone.

3. **Safety rules.** Establish and post house safety rules regarding the use of appliances, answering the door and telephone, and play activities.

4. **Emergency procedures.** Post emergency numbers and addresses on the phone. Make sure your child knows how to report emergencies. Practice emergency procedures and enroll your child in a community first aid or life skills class.

5. **Check-in.** Establish a check-in routine so that a responsible adult knows when your child has arrived home. If your child can't call you at work, he or she may need to check in with a neighbor.

6. **Friends.** Do not allow friends to visit your child when he or she is at home alone. Their unsupervised play may get out of hand. Be sure to build time into your family routine for other social interaction opportunities.

7. **Quality time.** Spend time with your child each day. Many children are fearful of staying alone and need an understanding adult to answer their questions and listen to their concerns.

8. **Entertainment.** Provide some type of safe home entertainment. Hobbies, a home computer, a 4-H project and simple chores are some ways to ensure that your child won't be bored after school.

9. **Travel.** Do not allow your child to experiment with new routes to and from school. If possible, have your child walk to and from school with friends. Counsel him or her to come straight home.

10. **Alternatives.** Keep looking for ways to provide adult supervised care. Work with your local PTA, recreation department or other community agency to establish a school-age child care program.

---

place. When worn around the neck, the house key advertises a child's vulnerability. The key should be kept on a chain or in a wallet, purse, or pocket. Children who carry keys should chain them around their necks or pin or tie them inside a pocket or belt where they are hidden from view. Never put your home address on the key chain in case it is lost. Under no circumstances should your child show or loan the key.

Some parents and children hide an extra key in case the original is lost. Creativity is needed in finding a good hiding place. The doormat and mailbox are poor choices. A loose brick or box buried in the shrubbery is a good choice in some instances. A safeguard is to leave an extra key with a trusted neighbor.

Getting Home

Instruct your child on proper safeguards to take en route to and from school. Even if your child ordinarily walks home or rides a bus with a particular friend, there is no assurance that the friend will always be present. Traffic safety, precaution with strangers, accident prevention, and entering a safe house are topics you should discuss with your child.

When children go to and from school on their own, certain strategies can ensure their safe arrival. It is important for your child to follow only those routes that you have agreed upon. Experimenting with short-cuts and accepting rides with strangers are dangerous. Tell your child to run to the nearest public place or safe house and ask for help if he or she is being followed by a stranger. Teach your child to detect signs of an intruder and when it is safe or unsafe to enter a house alone. If a window is broken, the door is open, or things don't look just right, your child should never enter the house. He or she should go to a neighbor's house instead. Setting up special role plays of home-alone situations and following them up with discussion can help your child learn to cope with unexpected events such as when it may be unsafe to enter the house alone:

> John comes up the steps to his house and sees the door standing open. "Mom must have come home early," is the first thought that pops into his head. What should John do?

Talking openly with your children about pretend situations will prepare them ahead of time for any situations out of the ordinary that they wouldn't otherwise be able to handle. Special problems that could erupt when older children supervise younger ones can also be rehearsed. Box 3–4 contains four problems that could happen when an older child is in charge of a younger sibling. Each problem also has five choices for solutions. You can help the older child practice by reading the problems, choosing the best solutions, and discussing why you arrived at the solutions you did.

Box 3-4 CARING FOR BROTHERS AND SISTERS

Read each problem and solution carefully. Circle the answer you feel is best.

Problem 1.

You and your brother are watching a television show and your brother changes the television channel and says, "It is my turn." What would you do?

Solutions:

a. Hit your brother and change the television channel to your show.

b. Call him a name.

c. Agree to let him choose the next show if you finish watching this one.

d. Call Mom or Dad.

e. Other

Problem 2.

Your little brother is bored and can't think of anything to play after he gets home from school. He complains to you, pesters you, and demands your help in finding something to do. What would you do?

Solutions:

a. Yell at him and tell him to leave you alone.

b. Try to talk to him.

c. Call your Mom or Dad.

d. Try to find a game to interest him.

e. Other

Problem 3.

After coming home from school, you and your little sister are to do homework. Your sister refuses to do so, laughs at you, and says, "You can't make me!" What would you do?

Solutions:

a. Get angry and yell at her.

b. Remind her of the home rules and consequences if she doesn't obey.

c. Grab her and physically make her stay at the homework.

d. Call Mom or Dad, or let them know when they come home.

e. Other

Problem 4.

You and your sister break a vase while wrestling in the living room. What would you do?

Solutions:

a. Agree with your sister not to tell your parents.

b. Tell your parents that your sister broke the vase.

Box 3-4   CARING FOR BROTHERS AND SISTERS (Continued)
c. Tell your parents you were wrestling with your sister and broke the vase.   d. Tell your parents you don't know how the vase was broken.   e. Other

Adapted from: Cooperative Extension Service/The University of Georgia College of Agriculture/Athens.

Check-ins

Children should go straight home from school, lock the door as soon as they get there, and call a parent to let them know they are home. Children should be told that if they plan to be later than usual, they should call you at work and tell the neighbor, if they ordinarily check in with that person. Check-ins allow both you and your child to feel more confident and put your minds at ease. Check-ins also allow you to avoid potential problems. Parents who work under demanding schedules need a creative check-in procedure. A child can call a parent's office and leave a message. Or a child can call the office three times in succession beginning at a certain time. With each call, the child allows the telephone to ring three times before hanging up. Obviously, this system has bugs. You may be called away at 3:25 or receive a business call between your child's second and third call. Parents who have access to a computer at work and at home can check in with their children using a telephone modem.

Telephone Skills

Adults and children must be careful of how they answer the telephone. Children at home alone are especially easy prey for those who abuse the telephone system. Anonymous or obscene calls or strangers asking personal questions can be dramatized through role play. Children should be taught to never tell an anonymous caller that a parent is not home. When someone asks your child to speak to a parent, for example, your child should be instructed to use such phrases as "Mom can't come to the phone right now" instead of "She won't be home until six o'clock.'' Obscene callers should be dealt with by hanging up immediately rather than attempting to identify the caller.

Many areas have telephone warmlines for home-alone children to use when frightened by callers or unusual sounds in the house or faced with emergencies. Your child should know this important telephone number if you have one in your vicinity. All essential telephone numbers—for the police department, fire station, poison control, parents' work, and nearest neighbor or relative—should be placed in a safe and accessible place for children to use in emergencies. Your child should practice finding and dialing these numbers swiftly, using the telephone book, and reaching the operator. We recommend a list of telephone numbers and names beside each agency, like the one in box 3–5. They will enable your child to act with haste and confidence when services are needed. For security reasons children should not be allowed to stay on the telephone for a long time. You and your child may want to agree on a time limit.

House Rules

Many parents feel a locked door is an important safety rule. But a home-alone child may feel more is needed. Young children are often afraid someone is hiding in a closet or under the bed. A child who includes these checks in the house rules will feel more secure.

Make sure you and your child agree on safety precautions and rules that must always be practiced in your absence. Almost all children we talk to report some sort of daily routine: changing clothes, getting something to eat, doing household chores, finishing homework, and watching television. A twelve-year-old boy shared his routines: ''I do my homework and then I do housework (trash, dishes, ashtrays, get wood, bathroom, fold clothes, sometimes wash then sweep) and watch TV.''

Most children have rules to follow, such as locking the front door, not using electrical appliances, staying inside, and not answering the door or telephone unless it's a parent's code ring. An eleven-year-old boy expressed comfort with these preparations: ''I've never been afraid by myself. I have a code to answer the phone only after two rings, and they call back. If it doesn't [ring twice], I don't answer it.''

One way to structure house rules is to help your child plan a daily schedule to use when he or she gets home. Daily routines help children

---

Box 3-5   HELP NUMBERS FOR KIDS*

Cut out and paste to cardboard. Hang or mount near the telephone.

Mom's   Work: _____

Dad's   Work: _____

Fire   Department: _____

Police: _____

Life   Squad/Ambulance: _____

Poison   Control   Center: _____

My City's Special Emergency Number: _____

Doctor: _____

    Office: _____ Home: _____

Hospital: _____

    Phone: _____

Neighbor: _____

    Phone: _____

My   Address: _____

Directions   To   My   House: _____

_____

_____

_____

---

*Adapted from the University of Georgia Extension Service.

Home-Alone Kids: The Working Parent's Complete Guide to Providing the Best Care for Your Child, Bryan E. Robinson, Bobbie H. Rowland, Mick Coleman (Lexington, Mass.: Lexington Books, 1989).

feel more secure being alone, especially in their first few days and weeks, and gives them a sense of control over their home surroundings. An example of one home-alone child's after-school schedule is shown here:

3:30	Arrive home	☐	Lock door
		☐	Check rooms and closets
3:30–3:45	Mom calls (Yea!)		
3:45–5:00	Free time	☐	Snack
		☐	TV, radio, telephone calls
		☐	Feed cat (please!)
5:00–5:30	Begin homework (Boo!)		
5:30–6:00	Mom arrives (Yea!)		

_____   _____

MOM'S SIGNATURE   DATE

_____   _____

JOHN'S SIGNATURE   DATE

The after-school schedule is simple and short. John's schedule provides direction without overloading him with details. Second, the schedule must be flexible. Large blocks of time give John ample time to complete all tasks. Third, humor makes the schedule less demanding. Some children may choose to decorate their schedules or place checks beside items they accomplish. The less imposing the schedule is, the more likely it will be followed. Finally, there is a space for Mom and John to sign and date the schedule. John's signature serves a dual purpose. It indicates that he helped develop the schedule and that he agrees to follow the routine.

The placement of the after-school schedule is important. Most school-age children head for the refrigerator as soon as they arrive home. The refrigerator door is an ideal spot for the schedule and other materials for your child. The map with names and telephone numbers of local agencies can also be put here if there is no room by the telephone. Another technique to remind home-alone children of house rules is to post a list of dos and don'ts. See box 3–6 for an example of the list to place next to John's afternoon schedule and a map of local agencies.

Box 3-6 JOHN'S HOUSE RULES

Do . . .   *Don't* . . .

- Use toaster
- Use fork and spoons
- Use the computer
- Play with train set
- Play in backyard when Ms. Jones is with you
- Plan weekend trip (John will plan meals, Jane will plan games)

- Use stove or oven
- Use knives
- Use Dad's electrical equipment
- Play with wood burning set
- Play outdoors, except backyard
- Fight with sister

_____   _____
MOM'S SIGNATURE   DATE

_____   _____
JOHN'S SIGNATURE   DATE

Notice that John's list has the same characteristics as his after-school schedule; it is simple, humorous, and signed. Also, for every "don't," there is a matching "do." Telling children what to do is more informative than giving the confusing command, "don't."

Emergencies

Mapping community service agencies and listing telephone numbers and names is the first step in helping a child respond to emergencies. Using the map and meeting service workers gives the child practice in implementing emergency procedures. A schedule for daily events and a list of dos and don'ts provide structure for home activities. Make sure your child has some understanding of first aid and can handle accidents. Your local YMCA and YWCA, Red Cross, and Scout organizations have first-aid and safety programs you and your child could take together. The twenty-step check will give you a final inspection of other areas for safekeeping.

The Twenty-Step Final Check

Take a final check before your child starts staying home alone. We have provided a checklist of twenty precautionary steps. If you have covered all twenty steps and feel your child understands and comfortably accepts them, then your family is ready for home-alone care.

1. Make sure your child understands why it is necessary for him or her to stay at home alone, how long it will be until you get home, how you will check on your child, and safety rules that are enforced.

2. Tape important numbers (office, the 911 emergency number, an at-home neighbor's number, police and fire departments, and poison control) and your address (work and home) to the telephone. Put other often-used phone numbers on the wall near the phone.

3. Teach your child basic first aid and select a specific location for a first-aid kit.

4. Help your child develop a daily routine to give some structure to after-school time. Go over safety rules including such basics as: don't climb on furniture, don't play with matches, don't use knives or kitchen appliances without an adult present, don't go to someone's house without permission, don't let friends inside to play or go outside to play with them unless you have permission.

5. Have your child call you each day when he or she gets home so you will know everything is okay and check in with an at-home neighbor if possible.

6. Encourage your child to talk about how he or she feels about being alone. A pet may be a good "friend" for companionship and also give your child a sense of security.

7. Call your child and let him or her know when to expect you if you plan to be later than usual getting home.

8. Make sure your child understands not to let strangers at the door know he or she is alone, not to let them inside the house for any reason, and not to go with a stranger even if the stranger says you sent them.

9. Give your child a set of house keys and a key chain with instructions to keep them out of sight. If your child wears a key on a yarn necklace, make sure it is worn inside the shirt. Visible keys ''mark'' a child who will be alone. Tell your child what to do if the key gets lost.

10. Make sure all locks in your home work and that your child knows how to lock windows and doors. *Always* keep doors locked.

11. Prepare your child for various phone calls by pretend telephone conversations. Tell your child not to say that he or she is alone. Your child should say you are busy and will call back later. If your child feels uneasy about the call, have him or her call you at work to talk about it. Be sure your child knows where a phone is if you do not have one in your house.

12. Make sure your child knows his or her full name, full home address, and phone number in case of an emergency.

13. Teach your child to get help in an emergency. Make sure he or she can use push-button and dial telephones, use the telephone book, call the operator, and make emergency, local, and long-distance calls.

14. Teach your child what to do in case of a fire. Hold practice fire drills showing exits and use of the 911 number. Install smoke detectors in your home. Children should know to leave the house if it sounds.

15. Let a neighbor know when your child will be staying alone so the neighbor can check on your child. If you do not have a home phone, ask a neighbor for permission for your child to use their phone in an emergency.

16. Have family meetings to decide matters such as house rules, any simple chores to be done, how much television may be watched, whether friends may come over, and under what conditions.

17. Discuss basic things to do in adverse conditions such as bad weather, power outages, and so forth.

18. Break daily routines by planning some after-school activities that your child would enjoy, such as Scouts, sports, or Y programs.

19. Provide safe snacks by putting them on a low shelf or table and furnish plastic cups and containers for juice. Let your child help plan healthy snacks. Make sure your child knows to clean up after eating.

20. Praise your child often for signs of maturity and self-reliance as he or she begins self-care. Your trust and praise will promote pride and responsibility.

Achieving the Delicate Balance

After reading the twenty steps, you can see you have a lot of teaching and your child has a lot of learning to do. But good, secure self-care requires time, thought, and preparation, and you will find all the planning is worth it in the long run. The other thing you may notice, looking over the list, is the amount of responsibility you are asking your child to take. It is important that the three R's—rules, routines, and responsibilities—are balanced with fun. You don't want your child to become a serious little adult.

Many school-age children find it difficult to leave interesting after-school activities and return to an empty house, and parents feel guilty about imposing rules that isolate their children from fun and friends. These problems can be eased by planning weeknight and weekend outdoor activities and quality times with your child. Enrolling your child in a weekend or after-school Y or local park and recreation department program is one way to meet social and physical needs. Nightly and weekend family outings and long walks and talks also help balance daily self-care obligations. Outdoor activities can be as simple as roller skating in the park with a friend or as elaborate as a fishing trip or family picnic to the zoo. Whatever the activity, the focus should be on giving children informal socializing time that they miss on weekdays.

On weekday evenings you can set up simple activities with your child that can be carried out around the house. The activities provide fun, learning, and parent-child interaction. You can find a wealth of resources in your everyday surroundings. One sample activity is "Measuring Around Objects." Instruct your child to find a number of objects throughout the house and measure around them with strings. Have them ponder which they think is the thinnest, fattest, and so forth. They then examine the lengths of the pieces of string and place the objects in order from thinnest to fattest. Finally they use the pieces of string to make a graph that can be darkened with different colored crayons and hung on the child's bedroom wall. You have just carried out a math activity with your child.

The following example provides a fun science activity:

Topic: Discovering Shapes That Float Best

Materials: Paper clips, ball of clay, water, cottage cheese container in which to store the paper clips and clay and to hold water for the activity.

Activities: 1. Change the ball of clay so that it floats.

2. Describe two shapes that float best.

3. Load the floating shapes with cargo (paper clips).

4. Record the amount of cargo each shape will hold before it sinks. The craft that carries the most cargo wins.

All activities should share certain characteristics. They should be educational as well as fun, often involving a game that can be repeated and enjoyed. They should appeal to a wide range of school ages and use common materials. Chapter 7 includes resources of after-school activities for children to do alone or with parents. The Boredom Busters in that chapter were developed especially for home-alone children.

Your role in your child's home-alone experience cannot be overstated. A fine line exists between letting children go or holding them too tightly to grow. Your child is entering settings where he or she can take care of him- or herself for a large part of the day. As this happens, your child feels a new sense of pride in work and achievements. For the most part children need little encouragement to develop a sense of industry and accomplishment. Both you and your child are now ready for a safe and exciting adventure!

4

How Are Your Kids Adjusting to Home-Alone Care?

I MAGINE you are eleven years old and home alone after school. You've taken the precautions set up by you and your parents and have settled down to finish your homework. A glass of milk, a chocolate-chip cookie, and the telephone are close by. You've checked in with your dad and called the neighbor across the street to let her know you're home safe and sound. You are among the throngs of children who find themselves home alone after school on a regular basis. You are one of the fortunate ones though, because you are *prepared*.

Safe and sound, that's the way it's meant to be. Feeling secure and knowing what to expect helps children in home-alone care without adding stress and anxiety.

Home-alone arrangements are as varied as the many different children who use them. As we mentioned earlier, younger children are being cared for by older brothers and sisters, some children are home without anyone, others check in with neighbors, and a few even spend time in the shopping mall or visiting friends.

Meet Charles, Vicky, David, and Carla, four kids in self-care who are practicing different degrees of self-reliance. They're making choices and learning to trust their circumstances. All of them have something to share with you. Their stories can help you understand the many needs of the child who spends time home alone. They can help you focus on your own child as you determine how your child is adjusting to being home alone.

Charles

Charles, seven, has a fourteen-year-old brother, a twelve-year-old sister, and a three-year-old sister. His father works out of town during the week, and his mother is a department store clerk who works most after-noons and Saturdays. Big brother lets Charles tag along when he plays in the nearby park, goes dirt-bike riding, or plays touch football with his friends.

Charles and his brother have rules they must follow, such as checking in with their mother by telephone. At times they are at odds with the older sister, who keeps her eye on their three-year-old sister after the sit-ter goes home at five o'clock. Their mother comes home a little after six and hurries to put supper on the table. There are good days and bad ones. As long as there are no emergencies, the children fare well. The day the older brother hurt his leg, Charles slipped and broke his collar bone, and baby sister ran a high fever and threw up all over the bed are examples of the stressful times.

Charles has to adjust to many authorities. He must please his big brother, his older sister, and his parents—a large order. At the same time, he is supervised and has a somewhat loosely tied safety net.

Vicky

Vicky, a third grader, comes home from school on the bus. Although tall for her age, she complains that the boys on the bus pick on her and that the driver is not much help. Her mother is a church secretary; her father died when she was five years old. Vicky stays home alone and lets herself into the house with her key. She is careful to lock the door behind her and to check through the house before she begins her home-work. Usually she makes herself a snack and watches television. Vicky says she is afraid sometimes at home alone because the house makes noises, and her imagination runs wild. She never plays outside when she is in self-care.

David

David, a fourth grader, goes directly to a neighbor's house to check in before he goes home. If he needs anything, he contacts the neighbor, who keeps a watchful eye on him. He can play outdoors, visit with friends, and have a snack left for him that morning.

Carla

Carla, a fifth grader who has been taking care of herself for years, does not go directly home. She stops at the park, goes by the shopping mall, and sometimes visits a friend. She does not like attending the day care center after-school program. She said it was for babies and cost too much money. Carla lives with her grandmother, who works at the neighborhood library. On cold or wet days, Carla spends her afternoons among the stacks of books. Although she enjoys reading, she would rather read in her own room, not in the library. When not in school, she spends more of her time alone.

No one knows your child better than you. Through the early childhood years you have learned the magic of your child. You have seen the best and the worst of this magnificent creature. You know how far to push, when to pull back, and when to leave alone. The parent-child relationship is dynamic and growing. It is special and cannot be duplicated by caregivers, extended family, or school teachers.

Because of this special relationship, parents such as you are best equipped to know how their children are adjusting to self-care. There are certain times when problems will arise. You can predict when and why problems are likely to occur by being atuned to your child's behavior and feelings. There are various ways of judging how your child is adjusting to self-care. Signs of stress and behavior changes that need immediate attention are just two signals of adjustment problems. We cannot emphasize enough the importance of spending quality time with your child. Interviews with children in self-care, research data, and personal experiences have showed us quality time together is the single most influential factor for developing positive home-alone arrangements.

From interviews with children in self-care, we found five levels of adjustment related to the length of time spent at home alone. It appears that children become more comfortable and secure as time goes by. There is some evidence that they might become complacent and, at times, even careless. An important task for you is to see that your child has a "safety shield," in fact and in attitude, that keeps him or her in touch with everyday realities.

Levels of Home-Alone Adjustment

Home-alone adjustment levels reflect how children feel about their arrangements and their success or failure. Some children are excited with their new responsibilities and decision-making opportunities. Others are fearful and apprehensive and work hard to create a brave front. More than half the children we interviewed said they liked or did not mind being alone and never had any fears. Most of these children lived in small towns or in suburban or rural areas outside small towns. The following quotes represent some of the children's comments:

"I'm okay." (ten-year-old boy)

"It makes me feel big." (eight-year-old girl)

"I've learned more responsibility." (nine-year-old boy)

"I like being alone because I can do anything I want to." (ten-year-old boy)

"It gives me time to think." (fourteen-year-old girl)

Of the children who liked being alone, some cited advantages of having parents at home in the afternoons:

"I wouldn't have to let myself in and don't have to worry about losing my key." (fourteen-year-old boy)

"I wouldn't have to clean as much and not have as much responsibility." (twelve-year-old girl)

"It would be great!" (fourteen-year-old girl)

"I could eat when I got home." (fourteen-year-old boy)

Older children who were unafraid had difficulty seeing any advantages of adults at home:

"It would be boring." (fourteen-year-old boy)

"I wouldn't have time alone to myself." (thirteen-year-old girl)

"I would have to start homework right then with no TV." (fourteen-year-old girl)

"I would have less time to myself and to talk to my friends on the phone because my parents won't let me use the phone when they are home." (thirteen-year-old girl)

"It would probably be a drag." (thirteen-year-old boy)

"I would have a hard time adjusting to them being home, and I wouldn't get to talk on the phone as much." (thirteen-year-old girl)

Not everyone was as positive. Many said they were frightened some or all of the time they were home alone. Fears usually were generated by such house noises as dishes settling against one another in the kitchen or the house creaking. Many of these children, though, admitted (without prodding) that even adults are sometimes uncomfortable hearing these noises. Following are a few other examples of what children shared with us:

"I'm afraid because there are wild dogs outside." (fourteen-year-old girl)

"Sometimes I feel like someone is always there." (thirteen-year-old girl)

"We have people call and play practical jokes." (fourteen-year-old boy)

"I'm afraid of being kidnaped." (twelve-year-old girl)

Level 1: Orientation

In the first level of self-care, children are preoccupied with survival. Normal house sounds, like creaking walls, or other sounds can cause fear in the beginning days of home-alone care. Children's imaginations will sometimes run wild until they get some experience. Children want to know the "dos" and "don'ts" of the situation. You help by establishing rules and teaching your child basic ways for dealing with the unexpected. Children at this stage occasionally forget to practice every rule, as eight-year-old Michael, who used to go to a day care center that "got kind of boring." He has been caring for himself for nine months and sometimes forgets to lock the door behind him.

Michael. When I get home at about three-ten, I get my key and go inside. Sometimes I lock the door, and sometimes I forget. I put my stuff in my room, turn on TV, and get something to eat. If I have homework, I wait till Mom gets home to do it. She gets home at about six. She usually calls me, though, at three-thirty to make sure I got in all right and that I'm okay. If I had a problem, I'd call her. She works at the bank, and I know her number by heart now.

After Mom calls me, I do my chores (clean up my room) and go outside and play with my friends. When it gets dark at home, I get kind of scared because I hear all these funny noises. Sometimes dishes will slide down and hit together, and that scares me. My imagination is really what scares me the most, because I think I see people running around in the house and stuff. But nothing bad's ever happened, and everything's going fine so far.''

Adjustment Evaluation. Michael has been caring for himself less than a year and is still somewhat negligent about routines. But he chose against a boring after-school program in favor of self-care even though he had to put up with scary sounds and his imagination. Clearly, Michael, not his parents, made the choice. Many children probably choose to care for themselves rather than attend inadequate programs. Apparently Michael decided that being with his friends after school was worth his apprehensions. His choice indicates that children have different degrees of fear. All school-age children are fearful at times, and even many adults feel uncomfortable alone when the house settles. Michael is too young to be alone, especially for such a long time. Although he has rules and routines, he often forgets to lock the door. Perhaps his negligence results from his young age or perhaps he just needs more time to learn the routines. Anchors that add to his secu-

---

Box 4–1 LEVELS OF HOME-ALONE ADJUSTMENT

1. **Orientation.** Children learn the ropes of their new arrangements.

2. **Questioning/Resentment.** Children question and may even resent the responsibilities they feel have been thrust upon them.

3. **Toleration.** Children tolerate their home-alone status, although they may often become bored.

4. **Acceptance.** Children have learned to accept and understand their self-care status.

5. **Appreciation.** Children at this level not only accept their lot, they also appreciate parental efforts.

rity are playmates and his mother's daily telephone calls to check on him. He seems self-assured that he could reach his mother in the event of a problem, and knowing her telephone number is a comfort.

Although Michael is still at the orientation level, by his own admission he seems to be adjusting extraordinarily well for an eight-year-old. As he adapts to the fears he identified, they will undoubtedly subside unless he is confronted with problems, such as obscene telephone calls, strangers at the door, or a traumatic accident. His confidence, or lack of it, in dealing with the unexpected could put him at another level.

Instruction and Guidance. You can help adjustment at this level.

- Ask your child to describe him or herself in self-care. For example, say, "Tell me about what you do when I'm not here." Children usually describe their activities and how they feel about the new experience.
- Provide your child with a journal and encourage daily entries to recall questions and concerns that come up when parents are not at home. Discuss the concerns. Write notes in the journal to remind your child of your love and support.
- Talk openly with your child about any apprehension about staying alone. Share your feelings and deal with your child's fears in constructive, positive ways. If there is a basis to the fear, fix whatever bothers your child. If it's a broken lock, for example, the fear can be remedied by repairing it.
- Be firm and insist that your child follow rules.

Level 2: Questioning/Resentment

During the second level children begin to compare their self-care experiences with the out-of-school arrangements of their friends. They question and even resent some of the rules. They may resent supervising younger siblings and being deprived of time with parents. Some children at this level may show signs of being emotionally immature for certain aspects of self-care. They may need detailed instruction on how to use their time alone. Eleven-year-old Sue and twelve-year-old Chuck are examples of children who are questioning their situations.

Sue. "When I get home at three-fifteen, I do light housework, start supper, and watch after my nine-year-old sister. We lock the door and stay inside until Mother gets home at five. She doesn't allow us to go outside for any reason. To tell you the truth, I don't mind cleaning and cooking, but I hate looking after my little sister. That should be for an older person to do. The only time I get scared is walking from the bus stop to home when my sister isn't with me."

Chuck. "Somebody called and wouldn't tell me who they were. I told them my dad was home, but he wasn't. When I called him to come to the phone, they hung up. I cried all afternoon. I called a neighbor to come stay with me and got out all the knives, a letter opener, a gun, and the fire extinguisher. My parents don't get home until after dark. I turn on all the lights and play Atari or something. I'm not with my parents much, except mornings and weekends. Kids whose parent are there when they get home get more done. They get to be around parents more and know about them and what they do. I'd rather not be alone. I wish my parents were home. But we get to do things together on weekends."

Adjustment Evaluation. Children at level two feel cheated; they feel that certain aspects of their arrangements are unfair. Sue resents supervising her younger sister and believes, perhaps rightly, that this is too much a burden for an eleven-year-old. Her only fear revolves around her responsibility for the nine-year-old's welfare. Chuck feels that children whose parents are at home in the afternoons have more advantages than he has. He misses being with his parents and feels deprived of knowing them better.

Some children at this level may not be emotionally mature enough for certain aspects of self-care. Sue does not mind her duties of cooking and cleaning, but the responsibility of another child is too much for her. Helping her move out of this level to another level, of toleration or acceptance, for example, might require removing the burden of sibling care.

Although a year younger than Chuck, Sue seems to be emotionally more prepared for her home-alone status. Chuck, on the other hand, does not seem to be adjusting well to any aspect of self-care. Anonymous telephone calls are traumatic for him, and he copes with them improperly: crying all afternoon and assembling an assortment of weapons. Emotionally, too, he seems to feel deprived of a special relationship that he needs with his parents. Helping Chuck move out of this level could require better preparation on how to handle problems. He needs instruction on how to handle anonymous calls. He also needs emotional reassurance from his parents, perhaps from better preparation to help him feel more secure. Chuck stated flatly that he would rather not be alone. Parents need to heed children when they utter such complaints. More time with his parents might help Chuck, or he may need a different arrangement altogether.

Instruction and Guidance. You can help adjustment at this level.

- Purchase story books especially written for home-alone children. These books help them with coping and safety skills and show them they are not alone. (See chapter 7.)
- Gather materials and supplies to stimulate new ideas and interests.
- Make special arrangements so your child can participate in outside activities of choice such as Scouts, dance or music lessons, and sports.
- Plan special outings for yourself and your child on weekends or your day off.
- Reevaluate your child's arrangement. Take the **HART** again in chapter 2. Ask yourself if you are being honest with your answers. If you rediscover that your child is emotionally overburdened, modify your current plan or explore other possibilities.

Level 3: Toleration

Level three can be called *toleration*. The child decides self-care is okay. Boredom can set in and the child may tire of regular routines. But the child learns to accept the situation and tries to make the best of it. Eleven-year-old Ralph does not like being by himself after school but has learned to tolerate his situation after five years as a home-alone child.

Ralph. "It's kind of boring, and it can get lonely at times when there's nothing to do. My parents work at night a lot—usually until about eleven-thirty. It scares me to be alone at night by myself. Somebody called one night and said my brother was in a wreck. They said he died in a hospital in the emergency room. I thought to myself, what would my dad think about it? When my dad told me it was a prank, it gave me a little confidence.

Dad took me out in the country and showed me how to shoot a .22 semiautomatic rifle. The reason my dad taught me to use the rifle is to be protective, so I won't worry if anything was to happen. He doesn't want me to mess with the pistol he's got because I might not be able to aim it as good as the other one (the rifle). It's the way my dad wants me to be, and that's the way his feelings are about it.

At night when I'm alone, I sit by the TV, and there's a gun rack above me so in case a robber came in or something was to happen, I'd be prepared for anything and I'd have a weapon to fight back.

I've managed it (self-care) for five years. It's not the best thing a kid would want to do. But when it comes down to it, it's the way I have to be. I can live with it and handle it. Overall, I'm pretty comfortable with the situation."

Adjustment Evaluation. Tolerant children no longer question their self-care arrangements but have learned to live with them. Although they have been in the arrangement for a long time, certain problems sometimes arise that lead to maladjustment, causing them to dislike being alone after school.

Ralph is alone for about eight hours, a long time for a child his age. He is bored and fearful. He lacks constructive ways of occupying his time; he seems to be idle. At night he is afraid of anonymous callers and intruders.

To help Ralph adjust better to his situation, his parents could help him find activities that capture his attention and interest. Ralph's fears probably stem from his father's poor attempts at preparation. Teaching an eleven-year-old to protect himself by firing a gun can instill more fear than it erases. The presence of firearms and instruction in their use tells children they have a lot to fear. Expecting such a young child to defend himself through such violent measures is an adult responsibility that is unfair and unhealthy for the child. A child who constantly wonders when and if he or she will have to kill someone will become emotionally strained. A parent who perceives a home-alone arrangement as life-threatening enough to equip a child with dangerous weapons should remove the child from it.

Ralph does not question or resent his father's survival skill tactics. Instead he sees it as the way things have to be. He sees no alternatives. Although he tolerates his position, Ralph does not cite any positive aspects of the arrangement. In his case, tolerance can mask deep-seated fears and resentments toward parents. Ralph's self-care situation is destructive. His parents need to instruct him on more positive ways of answering the telephone, adjusting to boredom, and coping with fears. They need to question their child's maturity level, reassess their own negative attitudes, rethink the amount of time they are leaving him alone, and make reasonable adjustments. We were not surprised to learn that Ralph is awaiting a court appearance to hear charges that he had illegal drugs—LSD and marijuana—in his possession.

Instruction and Guidance. You can help adjustment at this level.

- Focus on activities your child can do without help and take time to learn your child's favorite activities and interests.
- Emphasize enrichment and high-interest activities.
- Assist a child in choosing a project to work on and the needed materials and supplies while you are away. (See the Boredom Busters in chapter 7.)
- Select television programs in consultation with your child.
- Make lists, develop a schedule, create a calendar, and discuss each day's plan with your child.
- Communicate appreciation to your child for tasks well done and work accomplished.

Level 4: Acceptance

The fourth level, *acceptance,* finds the child confident in solving problems and enjoying a sense of security. The child knows what to do if a stranger knocks at the door, has the security of a next-door neighbor in the event of an emergency, and does not worry about the unexpected or unknown. Rex, an eleven-year-old, has reached this level.

Rex. "I don't mind being alone. I'm not afraid unless a stranger comes to the door. If somebody knocks that I don't know, I don't answer the door. I stay in my room. But I really don't worry about anything. My next-door neighbors are home most of the time, and we keep the key hidden most of the time. So I don't worry about losing it. Staying home by myself doesn't bother me at all. I like getting there (home) first. It makes me feel bigger, like I can do something by myself. I've learned that Mom and Dad can trust me."

Adjustment Evaluation. As a rule, children at the acceptance level have few worries, and, if they do worry, they feel confident that they can resolve problems. Rex doesn't mind being alone. He has several anchors of security: he knows what to do if a stranger knocks at the door; he has the security of his next-door neighbors in the event of an emergency; and unnecessary worry about losing a key was removed by establishing a safe hiding place for it.

Rex has been prepared so that he does not have to worry about the unexpected. Children like Rex who have accepted their status cite positive aspects of their arrangements. Rex, for example, likes getting home before his parents because it gives him self-confidence and a sense that his parents trust him. Apparently these payoffs outweigh the fear of a stranger coming to the door.

Instruction and Guidance. You can help adjustment at this level.

- Tell your child of your love, how proud you are when responsibilities are assumed, and that you have trust in his or her behavior and decisions.
- Leave notes in surprising places that remind the child of your love and care.
- Make frequent telephone calls on a regular basis to check on how things are going.
- Refrain from negative comments and nit-picking.

- Keep things pleasant and enjoyable.
- Emphasize your love and acceptance of the child and *don't* make acceptance contingent upon the way you would like your child to be.

Level 5: Appreciation

Level five, *appreciation,* occurs when self-care has worked fairly well for parents and children and there is a good feeling and a sense of accomplishment. Improved communication and mutual sensitivity exist between the parent and child, and self-care is not overly stressful. Children at this level not only accept their self-care arrangements but appreciate the benefits they and their parents get from the experience. This can be difficult for some children to grasp. It involves empathy and role-taking and calls for a degree of thinking that is usually found among children at eleven or twelve years of age. Eight-year-old Jennifer's views on her home-alone care are typical of this level.

Jennifer. "I've been going home by myself since I was in the first grade, and I'm in the third now. When I get home, I do my homework, wash dishes, and sometimes collect the garbage and dirty clothes and watch TV. If I have trouble with my homework, my mom helps me when she gets home. After I'm home an hour, my mom comes home. We watch TV together, or she goes upstairs and writes letters and I help. My favorite thing is to talk to her. I tell her how my day in school was and how I'm doing in school.

I have rules and stuff when she's not home. I lock the door behind me, can't use the phone, and can't go outside. I can't use any electrical things either—just the microwave—and can't answer the door. If somebody does come to the door, I just don't answer it. But I'm usually not scared 'cause there's somebody down the road that's home. It makes me feel big. I'm used to staying home alone. I stay inside the whole time. I do my homework at about three-thirty. I'm used to doing things at a certain time, but I don't have a certain schedule. I can't call Mom, and she can't call me because she works in a factory. But I know the numbers to call the police department or neighbor if I need to. They're up by the phone. But I've never had to call anybody. I like for my mom to work. She's always worked. If she didn't work, we wouldn't have anything."

Adjustment Evaluation. Children at this level have an appreciation for their parents' efforts. They also accept and appreciate their home-alone arrangements. Jennifer could not reach her mother in an emergency, but she has other safety nets: telephone numbers of neighbors and the police department. She also has the security anchor of rules and routines that she abides by in her mother's absence. And she has quality time with her mother every afternoon. They share open communication; she likes to talk to her mother about how things are going on a daily basis. Another security factor is that Jennifer has been caring for herself for two years, and she is alone for only one hour. Jennifer's one hour in the afternoon compared to Ralph's eight hours at night can make all the difference in the world in a child's adjustment when home alone.

Jennifer seems to be thriving from her self-care experience because she has been properly prepared. She has neighborhood and community support, and the amount of time she spends alone is realistic. Jennifer gets several payoffs as a home-alone child and expresses no fear. She enjoys the responsibility because it makes her feel big. She knows what is expected, feels she can manage the expectations, and expresses confidence in her brief time alone. She also appreciates her mother's working because she knows it is necessary. Most important, Jennifer has quality time with her mother to which she looks forward each afternoon.

Instruction and Guidance. You can help adjustment at this level.

- Spend quality time with your child daily.
- Share an open line of communication, talking daily about how things are going.
- Properly prepare your child to have several choices for dealing with the unexpected.
- Continue to read about, explore, and discover how children form their ideas about self-worth and competence.
- Encourage your child to get in touch with his or her feelings and share them.
- Encourage your child into new avenues of interest.
- Let your child know how appreciative you are of his or her role in helping the family function daily.

Adjustment Signs

Important questions have been raised about mental and emotional development of children in self-care. Questions are asked about fears and long-term resentment for having experienced independence and responsibility during the elementary years. If your child never moves beyond levels one and two, your self-care venture will not be positive. The first month in self-care is the most crucial. Here the foundation is laid for self-reliance and healthy, independent behavior. Careful attention to what your child is saying and doing will give you clues as your evaluation continues.

Ultimately, checks and balances between protection and preparation lie in your hands. You know your child best. Just as you notice changes in behavior when your child has a school problem or is coming down with a virus, you will be able to recognize changes regarding self-care. What signs tell you that your child is adjusting? How will you know if there are problems? Children may act out their poor adjustment through aggressive acts. They may block it through withdrawal, or they may be productive and industrious. How will you know where the energy is going? What are the symptoms and signs of adjustment problems? Box 4–2 lists ten signs that will alert you to trouble.

Understanding and recognizing these alert signs open doors for chil-

---

Box 4–2   ADJUSTMENT PROBLEM SIGNS

- ☐ Emotional upset and nervousness
- ☐ Difficulty sticking to rules and following directions
- ☐ Inability to handle sudden and unexpected events
- ☐ Increased anxiety and fear
- ☐ Expressed feelings of isolation, boredom, and loneliness
- ☐ Abrupt and uncharacteristic behavior changes
- ☐ Bad grades and unfinished homework
- ☐ Carelessness and irresponsibility
- ☐ Excessive stress
- ☐ Less quality time between you and your child

dren and parents. As problems surface, there are many ways to answer the call for balance and healthy adjustment. You can help your child develop coping skills and gain adequate knowledge to make self-care a positive experience. Children with successful self-care experiences perceive themselves as independent and capable. They like being alone. They are personable and well liked by their peers and adults. Their practices in self-management make them optimistic and enthusiastic about their role in the family.

Questions to Ask about Home-Alone Adjustment

You can ask yourself a number of questions that focus on how your child is adjusting to self-care. Take time to see how things are going and how your child carries out agreed-upon plans and follows established rules to help keep the home-alone situation in proper perspective. Monitoring your child's home-alone experiences is a daily exercise: By answering a series of questions, you can make a difference in the amount of frustration your child has being home alone. A "yes" to any of the questions means your child needs help adjusting in that area. If more than half of your answers are "yes," you may need to reconsider home-alone care.

1. Is your child having trouble adjusting emotionally at home alone after school?

   NO. Butch enjoys his newly found independence. He's proud of being responsible for himself two afternoons a week. The best part is no longer having to attend the day care after-school program. His habit of whining and pouting when he doesn't get his way has all but disappeared. He is eleven years old and experiencing a sense of competence and accomplishment.

   YES. Caroline telephones her mother at work several times each afternoon. She doesn't like being alone and has begun to bite her fingernails. Lately her homework is not complete when her parents come home from work and there is a struggle to get things finished before she drops off to sleep. Caroline needs some reassuring and another contact source to support her attempts at self-reliance.

Even though your child may not say he or she is upset or nervous at home alone after school, any of the following tell-tale signs can mean that emotional adjustment is not going well:

- nail biting
- sleeping difficulty
- irritability
- regressive behaviors such as "baby talk" or thumb sucking
- persistent clinging to you when you get home
- relapses in toilet training (for very young children)
- persistent fatigue or lethargy
- pouting or temper tantrums

2. Does your child have difficulty sticking to the schedule and rules that have been jointly established?

NO.   Curtis and his parents have agreed it is important to keep a close check on his routine when he is at home alone. He uses a check list to remind himself of tasks to be done. He signs and dates it when he's completed everything on it. In a sense he and his parents have a contract. Because Curtis is apt to become distracted with video games he has limited himself to thirty minutes' playing time each afternoon. He likes keeping up with the time and being trusted to regulate himself.

YES.   Marty and his mom have talked about the rules for staying home alone. He's to go straight home from school, stay inside and not invite any friends over. Marty does what he's told most of the time but occasionally he has friends in the house. He's careful to make them leave before Mom comes home. He knows he's breaking the rules and doesn't feel good about it, but "gets lonesome." Marty is twelve years old and is still in need of supervision.

Some home-alone kids have trouble sticking to rules and routines because they forget or become careless. Others knowingly and deliberately break the rules. You may discover this information when your child admits it or when a sibling or a neighbor tells you. You may discover clues when you get home that the house is messier than usual or your new vase is shattered into a million pieces.

When these clues do appear, be firm with the child but avoid a loud and harsh tone. Your child has given you a signal that he or she needs support. A calm, rational approach works best. Let the child tell you first why he or she broke the rule. Look at the reason behind the misbehavior and let that be the issue to work on, rather than focusing on the dirty house or broken vase. Once you discover the real reason for the rule breaking, jointly decide on how to remedy it. If the underlying reason, for instance, is boredom or loneliness, help your child with some of the Boredom Busters from chapter 7. If all else fails and your child continues to disregard rules and routines, look for alternatives to self-care.

3. Is your child helpless or unable to handle an emergency?

NO. The Jordan family has "practice" sessions dealing with emergencies on a regular basis. Sterling and his brother role play with mother how to call the 911 number and what to say when someone answers. They have placed a "Help Numbers for Kids" list on the refrigerator beside the telephone which contains all of the important emergency numbers.

YES. Brenda was cautioned not to cook when she was home alone. Brenda, fourteen years old, believed that she was perfectly capable of handling any type of emergency. The bacon was frying, the phone rang, and Brenda and her friend talked for a very long time. Suddenly she saw smoke coming from the kitchen. Brenda ran from the house, shouting, "fire, fire!" Fortunately, a neighbor was outdoors working in the yard. The neighbor entered the kitchen, used the fire extinguisher on the overheated grease and averted a house fire.

Some children seem to have more trouble than others with the unexpected. Children naturally adjust better when their lives are predictable and familiar. They are more secure when they know the rules and routines and what to expect each afternoon alone. Even when you think children are prepared for an emergency, their minds go blank as can any adult's. If your child has had an emergency or unexpected situation and fell apart or became helpless, you can give the youngster an anchor of security. The best approach is to talk calmly and reassuringly about what happened. Brainstorm about what the child could have done differently. Make a family game out of rehearsing situations such as when a stranger comes to the door, your child cuts her finger, or a grease fire gets started in the kitchen. Acting out such scenes in a lighthearted way can be fun and helpful. The child learns what to do next time while getting rid of emotions through laughter and playing. Remember that adequate preparation and rules eliminate the need for handling emergencies to begin with. Grease fires, for example, should never happen if parents have ruled out cooking and children follow the rule.

4. Does your child express anxiety and fear at being home alone?

NO.   Walker goes to Little League football practice at his elementary school playground. It's within walking distance of his home and he enjoys hearing the sound of his cleats as he walks home after practice. He lets himself in the house with his key, has some fruit and cheese, and then gives his mom a call. He is glad they let him come home alone. He likes being in charge of himself. It makes him feel big and important.

YES.   Bryan plays the radio at top volume. Being home alone makes him apprehensive and he hears every creak and shudder of the old, two-story house. He cannot break his habit of looking over his shoulder when he moves from room to room. His mother works to reassure him that the house is safe and that he is, too. Bryan needs this regular reassurance.

We have already discussed that many kids, even many adults, have some fear when they are alone at home, especially in the beginning. After a month or more, most children get used to being alone and irrational fears evaporate. Bothersome signs that could surface are when the child dreads going into an empty house, has nightmares, seems more tense than usual, or calls you incessantly at work over a "strange" noise in the house. If your child still harbors fear or worry after one month, you will need to reevaluate your home-alone arrangement.

5. Does your child's home-alone arrangement lack adult contact or a check-in system?

NO. Laura comes home from school each afternoon and enjoys staying alone. She likes her privacy and the quietness of the house. She has telephone numbers in case of an emergency and has recently learned about the after-school helpline number. She has called it only once. The person who answered was friendly and encouraged her to talk. Mainly she was lonely and it made her feel good to hear another voice. It is not unusual for Laura to feel lonely or bored at her age (twelve years old). She needs a chance to talk to adults during the afternoon. It makes her feel "supervised."

YES. Sally feels isolated when she is home alone after school. Unfortunately their telephone has been disconnected, and her mom has instructed her to stay inside. She has the television to occupy her and does her homework on a regular basis. One afternoon a man came to the door and knocked several times. It seemed like an eternity to Sally, and she did not answer his knock. Eventually he left. Sally knows it's silly to be afraid of every stranger who comes to the door. But she has been told to keep herself hidden and not to let anyone know that she is home alone. Her teacher talked about it, her mom reminds her each day, and some of the television programs caution against strangers. She wishes she could talk with someone about her fears. She does not want to bother her mother when she gets home from work. Mom has enough to worry about. Sally is taking on one of the disturbing characteristics of some home-alone children. She is not dealing openly with her feelings and doubts. She needs an "adult" listener.

A home-alone arrangement requires ongoing and active participation at every level. It requires daily evaluation and re-evaluation on your part. Children need adult contact while they are home alone, even if it is a telephone call, so that they "feel supervised" and cared for. They need a willing ear to listen to problems or concerns they have about being alone. At some point in the evening, parents can show an interest in their children by asking how their day and afternoon went. Most importantly, spending quality time with your child is the single most influential factor for developing positive adjustment in self-care arrangements.

6. Have your child's attitude and behavior toward school, friends, or family changed abruptly?

NO.   If anything, Lynn is more enthusiastic than ever about school. She likes staying home alone and at twelve years old she compares her status with that of her friends. They are not as independent as she is and certainly don't have as much freedom. At times she feels as if she's years older than they are. They seem immature and childish. Lynn thinks her parents are the best for letting her stay alone. She is responsible, quiet, and prefers indoor activities. This type of mature child is the best candidate for successful home-alone care.

YES.   Lisa (age fourteen) had never been an "A" student, but she had kept up with her studies and taken pride in her work. She began to distance herself from her best friends when her grandmother moved back to Texas and left her to care for her younger sisters. Her friends offered to come over to help her baby-sit but she discouraged them. Now they go on their way and Lisa feels left out and isolated. Imagine her mom's surprise when she got a call from the school principal who told her that Lisa had skipped school. It seems that Lisa had joined another group of kids who were in trouble quite often. Mom confronted Lisa with the problem, and they worked it out together. Mom hired a sitter for the two younger kids and Lisa is free to run around with her old buddies.

If your child has been even-tempered, cooperative, and fairly careful and suddenly begins to behave aggressively or out of character, he or she is sending a signal that something is wrong. Examples of extreme changes are:

- hitting without cause
- yelling threats
- picking on little brother or sister
- sulking
- uncommunicative at meals
- excessive daydreaming
- watching television constantly
- sleeping excessively

- overeating
- lateness
- carelessness

If your child has been happy and likable and then begins to see himself or herself as helpless or inferior, extreme changes such as these might be observed:

- becomes sullen
- is unusually sad
- worries excessively
- is irritable and hard to get along with
- acts confused
- is demanding
- has unfounded fears
- becomes frustrated easily
- talks of being lonely
- has little confidence
- doesn't try new things
- lacks enthusiasm

Sudden changes in your child's normal behavior are reason for concern. Your child is telling you indirectly that something is wrong. You need to talk openly about the changes you have noticed and how you feel about them. Try to find their origins and see if they are related to the home-alone experience. If your child feels overly burdened with the new responsibilities, see that some of them are removed. If your child is angry at you because he or she doesn't get enough of your time and attention, plan special outings that both of you can look forward to on evenings or weekends when you can spend family time together. Take steps to resolve the problem by talking it out and making alterations wherever possible.

7. Have you noticed problems with grades or homework completion?

NO.   Chris has changed his homework habits since being in self-care. He tries to finish all the assignments before his parents get home so he can watch TV after supper. His mom and dad don't allow TV watching if there's work to be done. Before Chris was in self-care he was in the day-care after-school program. It was just too noisy to concentrate, and he likes staying at home alone much better. If he runs into a problem, the local school system provides tutorial services for kids needing help with homework.

YES.   Chip is beginning to act out his frustrations of self-care by getting into trouble at school. He doesn't finish his homework. The teacher has sent several notes home. Chip's parents have scolded, threatened, and even bribed him with promises of money if he goes for three days without an incident. Chip needs careful attention. He's confused about what is expected of him and his parents are not modeling consistency or ways to express feelings.

Grades that nosedive or homework that doesn't get finished is a clear indicator that home-alone care is interfering. A drop in grades could mean that children lack confidence in the ability to stay alone and dwell on their apprehensions rather than concentrating on class lessons. Some kids who don't use their time well in the afternoons put studying on the back burner, behind television or talking on the telephone.

Your child's self-confidence should improve after the first month with your continued support and reassurance. Talk about how to manage time and make firm rules about no television until after homework. Encourage your child to do as much schoolwork alone as possible until you get home from work. Then set aside a block of time when you can help with individual personal attention. Some days your child will have finished homework, and you can use the time to enjoy each other's company. Other times your youngster will just want to have you nearby in case questions come up about an assignment.

Some neighborhoods have established telephone helplines to assist home-alone kids with their homework after school. These programs are staffed by senior citizens and high school students, and have been an asset and can be replicated in your community (see chapter 6).

8. Are there signs that your child is becoming lax or careless in following rules?

NO.   Terri has made a chart of "house rules" and posted them in the kitchen. She knows the rules by heart, but having them inside is a good reminder for her. Terri likes to read, play the piano, and paint. The time she spends alone usually is filled with these activities. Instead of becoming lax she has become more dependable and is pleased when her mom compliments her for being extra careful and following the rules. Children who are responsible, quiet, and prefer indoor activities are at less risk than those who are argumentative, independent, and prefer the outdoors.

YES. The rules are posted. No cooking, no leaving the door unlocked, no kids over, no strangers in the house, etc. The list goes on and on. The longer Cindi stays alone the less strange taking care of herself has become. She knows the rules are important but things are OK. And she's not as careful as she used to be. Yesterday, for the second time this week, Mom found the front door unlocked when she came home from work. Cindi was in her room reading. Mom was furious. Cindi wants to remember but gets careless sometimes. They will have to establish some check points to help Cindi remember the rules. A call from Mom or a neighbor to see that Cindi has locked the door and is following the other rules will help. Elementary-age children need reminders and a feeling of being supervised even if from afar.

Nobody's perfect. Children are not adults and we cannot expect them to be. No matter how well you have prepared your child, there will be relapses. Expect it to occur, especially in the beginning stages of self-care. Rules are broken in the beginning because children don't have them down. Other times they are broken after years into the experience because kids become complacent. How many times have you left your keys in your front door when bringing in an armful of groceries? When children get careless, try to refrain from anger and from being too harsh. It only intensifies their frustration. But don't overlook their carelessness. Firmly and lovingly point out their laxness. Let them know the seriousness of their infraction and calmly remind them of the agreed-upon rules.

9. Are there any signs of stress?

NO. John and Jim are twin sons of a local doctor. Since preschool they have been a handful. They convinced their parents they could handle staying home alone. From the first it was exciting, and time flew by. Their parents knew the twins would need limited supervision, so they arranged for a check-in system with a neighbor. The boys go to the neighbor's house upon arrival from school and have a snack. They go to their house down the street and stay until their parents come home from work. If there is a problem, the neighbor is nearby. So far, so good.

YES.   Mary Louise had been complaining of a stomachache on the days she had to stay home alone. Because she's tall for her age, her parents tend to forget how vulnerable she is. There were other signs of her stress. She cried easily and had become quite moody. Fortunately for Mary Louise, her mother arranged after-school care with a neighbor. She goes directly to the neighbor's house and has become more pleasant and feels much better than she did before.

Stress can come from lots of places in children's lives. It's possible that children will show signs of stress that are totally unrelated to being home alone. You may notice minor signs that appear immediately after home-alone care starts. After about one month, minor signs of stress subside. But if stress signs are multiple and continue to escalate, you must intervene.

If your child has been physically active and in good health and then frequently becomes ill or fatigued, be on the lookout for:

- frequent stomachaches
- headaches and body aches
- persistent tiredness
- lack of energy in mornings
- the need to be prodded
- nervousness
- finicky eating, picking at food
- restlessness
- disrupted sleep
- school phobia
- weight loss

Never start children in self-care while your family is under crisis or stress. The death of a close family member, move to a new neighborhood, or separation or divorce are all stressful events that can heighten tension when children begin staying home alone.

10. Has the quality time you spend with your child decreased?

NO. Barbara Jordan carefully plans weekend activities for the family. She checks newspaper listings of upcoming events and shares the many available options with her two sons. Together they choose what they'll do. They visit parks, take in concerts, eat hot dogs, and spend a lot of time in the hands-on science museum. Each weekend is full of exciting events. Barbara also saves time for talking and listening. Sterling and Nicholas have a lot to share about school and friends. They are home-alone kids with a full-time, working, single mother. Barbara is pleased with their adjustment. There are problems but nothing that cannot be worked out with everyone's self-esteem intact. Her quality time doesn't happen by accident. It is carefully planned and attended.

YES. There's too much homework to catch up on in the Martin home each weekend. Sylvia Martin, a single parent, spends all day Saturday cleaning, shopping, and cooking. The kids, Bill and Jim, pitch in to do their share. But they're just kids and can't do some of the heavy work. There are times when Sylvia wants to give up. Bill and Jim fight a lot. They run in and out of the house slamming doors. She yells. It's a constant strain on everyone. Sylvia could use some physical and emotional help. Some communities have support groups where parents share their stories and learn new ways of coping.

Hopefully, after all we have said, you have grasped one point more than any other. As children begin to stay home alone, you plan and spend more quality time with them. Children need their parents' undivided attention every so often. Parents who work find it easy to get caught up in paying bills, bringing home extra work, civic obligations, or keeping their social life active to the exclusion of their children. Being sensitive to the balance children need in their daily lives is crucial for successful home-alone adjustment.

Eliminating Family Stress

Self-care, by nature, can lead to stress for parents and children. Many times parents are under stress and don't even know it. Parents rush to work in the mornings, put in a full day, rush home to take children to lessons, rush back to pick them up, rush home to prepare dinner (or grab a bite out), rush to an evening meeting, and rush back to get the children in bed. Children rush to school in the mornings, rush home (or to music lessons, Scout meetings, or after-school programs) in the afternoons, hurry to get their homework and household chores completed, grab a bite to eat, and collapse after a full day of work.

Parents, teachers, and the principal of an affluent private school recently told us that the stresses on their children are overwhelming. Everyone is afraid to let up for fear of being criticized. Parents said children bring the stress on themselves because they are competitive and want to keep up with one another. "Kids compete with each other," said one mother. "We don't pressure them." Some children have weekly schedules that would make a top corporate executive appear lax. One mother said her child has no time to play during the week: "My child has a full weekly schedule of club meetings, dance classes, music lessons, Girl Scouts, and cheerleading practice. In between she has tons of homework every evening. And she's not willing to give up anything for fear of being left behind!"

Teachers blamed parents and said they needed to let up. Parents complained that teachers overload children with too much homework. One teacher responded, "If we reduce the work load, then parents will criticize us for not doing our jobs." The principal complained, "If we let kids play, when will they learn?"

Because no one is willing to take responsibility for imposing stress, the cycle continues. It is the parents' responsibility to intervene on behalf of their stressed children. The best way to do that is to create, where possible, a stress-free family climate. You will find the following suggestions useful:

1. Do not hurry your children. Let them grow and develop at their own pace, according to their unique developmental timetables.

2. Encourage children to play and do things children do. Some of our fondest memories are of our childhood experiences.

3. Do not force-feed learning. Have reasonable expectations based on what children are capable of performing at their respective ages.

4. Let children have some daily and flexible schedule at home with free time built in for choosing from activities that match their interests.

5. As much as possible, protect children from the harsh pressures of the adult world, with time to play, learn, and fantasize.

6. As much as possible, provide children a peaceful and pleasant home atmosphere, shielded from excessive marital disputes and parental conflict.

7. Try not to pass your stress on to your children. Give them opportunities to talk about their own worries and stresses.

8. Guide children toward wise decision making by introducing limited choices that match their emotional maturity.

9. Reward children for their triumphs and successes, no matter how small. Let them know you love them and are proud of them for who they are and not who you want them to be.

10. Start the day on a positive note with pleasant words and calm routines.

11. Plan special times together each week as a family (without television), and listen to what your children have to say.

12. If you push your child, ask the question, "Am I doing this for my own ego or the child's benefit?"

The period of childhood, compared to adulthood, is the shortest time in the life span. Some children burn out before they have lived through this brief period. Childhood lays the bedrock for adult lives, and youngsters who have a chance to be children will become healthier, more well rounded adults.

Building Family Life

Home-alone kids stay by themselves a lot because one or both parents work. Children who care for themselves regularly deserve a reward occasionally for a job well done. One of the best gifts of appreciation parents can give is to build family strengths. By that we mean taking special care to plan a few evenings together as a family. Preparing meals together and having pleasant conversations at mealtime (without television) give families with home-alone kids a chance to communicate.

Discuss with your children the nature of your job. Let them know where you go and what you do all day long. Listen to what they have to say, too. Find out what they have been up to during the week. Avoid too much television watching as a family, and save newspaper reading until the children are asleep. Plan time with youngsters by helping them with homework, playing board games, scheduling weekday or weekend family outings, or conducting family projects. Start the day on a positive note with pleasant words and calm routines. Sometimes this might mean getting up fifteen minutes earlier so the family is not rushing to get out the door. Make your home a secure place where children can be alone, happy, and safe.

Do not make snap judgments and criticize children unnecessarily. Every situation has a positive and negative side. Try to focus on the positive things children do rather than always harping on the negative. This is not to say that children should not be disciplined, only that they should not be used as scapegoats when parents are tired. Do not spend all your time working. Limit the amount of work you bring home in the evenings and on weekends. Save some of that time for special moments with your most precious resources, the children. Do not come home in a foul mood. Children have bad days, too. Try to unwind and set a pleasant tone for family evenings. Do not make a habit of leaving your children at home a lot in the evenings and on weekends; they already spend most of their time home alone. Be sympathetic to their needs. Limit the number of times you go out, or take them along whenever possible.

Making the Best of Home-Alone Care

The adjustment problems children have from home-alone arrangements depend on your attitude toward self-care and the degree to which you prepare your child for this experience. Guilt, worry, and uncertainty may be your overriding emotions, but channeling these feelings into positive actions can improve an otherwise difficult experience for you and your child.

Scrutiny of the existing family climate is important, too. By eliminating unnecessary stress and tension where possible, your family will function more smoothly. A searching and fearless inventory of your attitudes about self-care and feelings of guilt and uncertainty might uncover subtle influences on how your youngster is adjusting.

Once you take these actions and provide the best child care possible, give yourself a break, worry less, and make the best of your situation.

5

How Can You Balance
Your Work and
Home-Alone Care?

D oes the following daily routine sound familiar?

8:00 AM – 9:00 AM   Rush to work.

9:00 AM – 3:00 PM   Put in a full day's work.

3:00 PM – 3:30 PM   Rush to call child from office phone.

3:30 PM – 5:00 PM   Finish up the day's work, wondering if child is okay.

5:00 PM – 7:30 PM   Rush home to take child to after-school activities.

7:30 PM – 8:30 PM   Rush home to prepare dinner.

8:30 PM – 10:00 PM   Rush to complete household chores before bedtime.

Working parents have told us over and over that they feel like they are walking a tightwire between balancing home and work life. We are frequently asked, ''Where is family time?'' Where, indeed! This question has come to reflect what we repeatedly hear as a growing frustration for working parents, especially those with home-alone children. One working mom described the stress associated with her work and child's self-care situation in the following way.

If it's not one thing, it's another. I spend all my time either working to provide for my family, worrying about the safety of my child who is at home alone, or feeling guilty about neglecting my family. There are some days when it's enough to drive me crazy.

It is no secret that today's stress level is high for working parents. If you are like this working mom, you constantly try to cope with family and work without the added pressures of worry and guilt. You no doubt also receive little help. Another working mom told us of her frustration in balancing her work and family life.

I keep looking for good after-school care for my child, but it's not to be found—at least around here. I sometimes wonder if anyone really cares about me or my child.

Sound familiar? Working parents of home-alone kids frequently voice feelings of being out of control. They complain that work schedules and civic responsibilities are decided with little regard to family time, and that society in general sends them a message that it is their job to adjust their family life as best they can. In the meantime, they continue to hope and search for help.

Is there help? The answer is "yes!" You can take charge of your life and that of your family. The information that follows can help you to accomplish this seemingly impossible feat by developing a plan to discover the balance in your work and family life and to build those areas you find weak. The three life areas that make up your action plan are: (1) your school-age child; (2) your family; and (3) your work life. The way in which you balance these three life areas will show how well you are coping.

Work and Family Life: A Tightwire Act

As a working parent, one way to view your life is to imagine it as a circle that is made up of the three life areas (your child, family, and work life). Each life area should be of equal importance if your life circle is to keep its shape—its balance. Box 5-1 will tell you how well you do at balancing your work and family life.

Box 5-1   YOUR LIFE CIRCLE

In each blank write the number that fits how true each of the following statements is of you: 1 = Strongly disagree; 2 = Disagree; 3 = Agree; 4 = Strongly agree.

Area 1: Your Child

_____ 1. "I carefully plan time into my day to be with my child."

_____ 2. "My child and I are as close today as ever."

_____ 3. "For fun, my child and I choose activities that we both enjoy."

_____ 4. "There is a mutual degree of respect between me and my child."

_____ 5. "My child and I negotiate house rules."

_____ 6. "I provide my child with an abundance of praise."

_____ 7. "My child is an independent thinker."

_____ 8. "My child is good at solving problems that arise when at home alone."

TOTAL _____ CHILD SCORE	*Add the numbers in the blanks and write your score in the space to the left.*

Area 2: Your Family

_____ 1. "The members of my family are good communicators."

_____ 2. "The members of my family are supportive of one another."

_____ 3. "The members of my family share household responsibilities equally."

_____ 4. "My family has a positive outlook on life."

_____ 5. "The members of my family are free to be whoever they want."

_____ 6. "My family plays together regularly."

_____ 7. "My family has deep spiritual beliefs."

_____ 8. "My family is good at facing problems head on."

TOTAL _____ FAMILY SCORE	*Add the numbers in the blanks and write your score in the space to the left.*

(Box continued)

Box 5-1   YOUR LIFE CIRCLE (Continued)

Area 3: Your Work

_____ 1. "My work and family life are in perfect harmony."

_____ 2. "I have interests outside my work duties."

_____ 3. "I rarely socialize with my work colleagues after work hours."

_____ 4. "I enjoy my work today just as much as ever."

_____ 5. "I work overtime only on very special occasions."

_____ 6. "I am able to leave work at the office."

_____ 7. "I am good at organizing my work time."

_____ 8. "I say 'no' to extra duties that take away my personal time."

TOTAL _____ WORK SCORE	*Add the numbers in the blanks and write your score in the space to the left.*

Scoring: Your life circle (figure 5-1) is made up of three parts: (1) your child; (2) your family; and (3) your work. To see how well you are balancing your life circle follow these steps:

1. Place an "X" over the number on the "child" part of the circle that matches your "TOTAL CHILD SCORE." Then darken in the "child" part of the circle up through the number on which you placed an X. For example, if your "TOTAL CHILD SCORE" is sixteen, then put an X over the number sixteen in that part of the circle marked "child." Then darken in the "child" part of the circle between eight and sixteen.

2. Repeat these steps for the FAMILY and the WORK parts of the circle.

Interpretation: To assess the balance in your life, look at your circle. What part of the circle is most complete—the child, family, or work area? This is the part of your life to which you devote most of your energy. Is there an area of the circle that is less complete than the others? This is the part of your life that needs more attention.

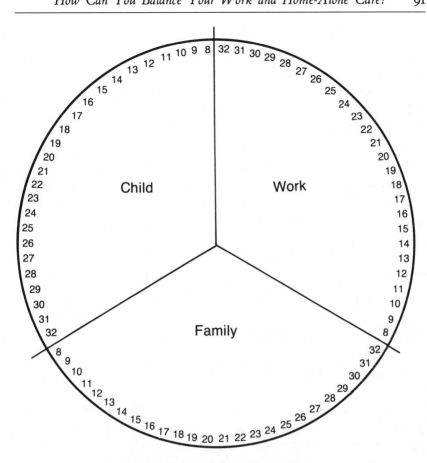

Figure 5–1. YOUR LIFE CIRCLE

Knowing the balance in your life is the first step to developing an action plan. You function best when you are able to juggle the interests of your child, family, and job. Without this balance you may find something missing or find yourself under stress. Taking time to develop a balance between all three areas of your life circle will ensure more harmony at home, at work, and at play.

Before looking at ways to do this, it will be helpful to consider some of the unique challenges facing parents with home-alone children. Knowing you are not alone in your concerns will make the following suggestions more meaningful.

Family Development During the School-Age Years

Families, like individuals, change over time. They expand with the birth or adoption of a child and shrink when adult children leave the nest or when divorce or death takes a family member. Families with school-age children are in a period of great expansion because children start school. And with school comes a whole new world of opportunities, experiences, and challenges.

As a parent of a school-age child, you must face the fact that your child is influenced more and more by peers and teachers. Your child also may pressure you for more independence. All this means that trying to remain in control of your child's behavior is impossible. One parent summarized the pressure of having a school-age child this way:

He's not my little boy anymore. He gets embarrassed if I try to kiss him goodnight, and his clothes—his clothes are just awful! But I've given up trying to change his taste in clothes. After all, his friends now set the fashion standards, not me.

Sometimes it's hard, but being a parent of a school-age child means letting go.

The family budget is another life challenge for parents of school-age children. Money gets tighter as children enter school, with the economic strains of buying school clothes (the *right* school clothes, as defined by your child's peer group) and supplies. You probably are also putting aside money to pay for your child's enrollment in sporting activities and youth clubs.

Finally you may be experiencing the physical stress of parenthood as a result of the rushed nature of your daily routine. The Parenting Stress Profile (box 5–2) will reveal your stress level and the types of stresses you have.

No one said being a working parent is easy. Being a child at home alone is not always easy, either. Your stress level, and that of your family, comes back to the life circle. Knowing how to balance the needs of your child, family, and employer can make your life less stressful and build your family strengths.

Box 5-2 PARENTING STRESS PROFILE

Place a "1" in the space beside each symptom that you have noticed in yourself during the past month.

Physical Stress

_____ Headaches	_____ Teeth grinding
_____ Fatigue	_____ Insomnia
_____ Weight change	_____ Restlessness
_____ Colds or allergies	_____ Accident-prone
_____ Pounding heart	_____ Upset stomach
_____ Tension in muscles of neck or shoulders	_____ Increased alcohol, drug, or tobacco use

TOTAL PHYSICAL _____ **STRESS SCORE**	*Add your scores. Write your score in the space to the left.*

Mental Stress

_____ Forgetfulness	_____ Confusion at home
_____ Dulling of the senses	_____ Poor concentration
_____ Decline in problem-solving skills	_____ Loss of creativity
_____ Lowered productivity	_____ Boredom
_____ Negative attitude	_____ Mental exhaustion
_____ Errors in judgment	_____ Confusion at work

TOTAL MENTAL _____ **STRESS SCORE**	*Add your scores. Write your score in the space to the left.*

Emotional Stress

_____ Anxiety	_____ Irritability
_____ Feeling "uptight"	_____ Depression
_____ Mood swings	_____ Nervous laughter
_____ Constant worrying	_____ Self-criticism
_____ Bad temper	_____ Crying spells
_____ Loss of interest in hobbies	_____ Easily discouraged

TOTAL EMOTIONAL _____ **STRESS SCORE**	*Add your scores. Write your score in the space to the left.*

(Box continued)

Box 5-2   PARENTING STRESS PROFILE (Continued)

Social Stress

_____ Isolation	_____ Lowered sex drive
_____ Resentment of others	_____ Nagging others
_____ Loneliness	_____ Being impatient
_____ Lashing out at family	_____ Clamming up
_____ Lashing out at friends	_____ Using people
_____ Lashing out at co-workers	_____ Being vindictive

TOTAL SOCIAL _____ **STRESS SCORE**	*Add your scores. Write your score in the space to the left.*

Scoring: Because we are unique, we have different levels of stress and different kinds of stress symptoms. To determine how much *physical, mental, emotional,* and *social* stress you have, follow these steps:

1. Write your *physical, mental, emotional,* and *social* stress scores in the blanks on the grid on page 95 (figure 5-2).
2. Put an "X" on the line above each stress symptom that matches your score. For example, if your *physical* stress scores is six, then put an X on the vertical line that is across from the number six.
3. Repeat step 2 for your *mental, emotional,* and *social* stress scores.

Interpretation: Review your stress scores on the grid. What stress symptoms are most common? Compare your scores to those of your family members. Plan a family meeting to discuss the different levels of stress within your family. Consider the reasons for the stress found in your family and think of ways to reduce it. Most regions of the country offer stress-reducing classes through local community colleges and universities, mental health centers, churches, and county cooperative extension offices.

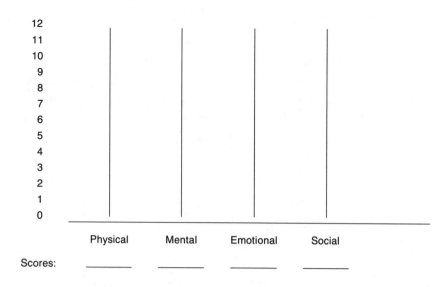

Figure 5–2. PARENTING STRESS GRID

School-Age Children and Your Life Circle

All kids want to feel safe, important, cared for, and loved by their parents. Children whose needs are met are better able to protect, care for, and love others. But when these needs are not met, children find it difficult to give to others what they themselves never experienced. Therein lies a source of great concern to many working parents who fret that self-care responsibilities may lead children to feel unsafe, unimportant, uncared for, and unloved. In a way, such concern is justified, because a self-care home can never be judged as safe as one with adult supervision. Home-alone care prevents children from interacting with parents and peers after school during important pastimes such as games, sports, and clubs. These activities contribute to children's sense of personal value and identity with peers.

Although peers and teachers are important in your school-age child's life, you remain the most important source of support and comfort. Two of the best ways to balance your child's home-alone care is to arrange for quality time and to use planned discipline.

Quality Time

The term "quality time" has been around for a long time. Yet, the concept is often misunderstood. The problem comes when parents define quality time as the amount of time they spend with their child in a busy activity. In fact, quality time is not defined by the amount of time you spend with your child but by the types of activities that take place during that time. Consider the following situations.

Situation #1

Joan, mother of an eight-year-old, estimates that she spends six "quality time" hours with her daughter each day between the time school ends and bedtime. Joan is proud of her homemaker role. She cleans the house weekly and always has meals prepared on time. To maintain her perfect home, Joan spends her afternoons washing clothes and preparing dinner while her daughter finishes homework and plays outside. After dinner, Joan immediately washes the dishes, finishes ironing, and works on quiltmaking. Meanwhile, Joan's family watches television.

Situation #2

Sue, mother of an eight-year-old, works full-time. Because Sue does not get home from work until between six and seven, she spends two to three hours each evening with her son before bedtime. Unlike Joan, Sue doesn't worry too much about her household chores getting done on time. Dinner also is late on those evenings when traffic is slow. After dinner, Sue doesn't immediately wash dishes. Instead, she waits until later in the evening when her son can help. Sue prefers to spend the time after dinner taking walks with her husband and son, or talking with her son about the day's activities.

Who spends quality time with her child? The answer, of course, is Sue. Although Joan spends *more* time at home with her child, she spends little of that time *with* her daughter. Joan and her daughter do not talk. Sue, on the other hand, spends little time at home with her son, but she makes that time count by playing and talking with him.

Quality time is easy with a little planning and creativity. Try the following.

1. *Plan for quality time.* Quality time does not automatically happen. Work schedules, family obligations, social demands, and civic duties can eat away at what little free time you have to spend with your child. This makes it necessary for you to plan for some parent-child time each day by marking it on your calendar, or, better yet, committing to a time as a matter of daily practice.

2. *Engage in quality activities.* Quality activities are those things that involve just you and your child. Parents often view quality activities as either expensive or demanding. But most quality activities take place at home and are inexpensive. Talking and listening to your child, playing a game, gardening, going on a walk or bike ride are some of the simple but "quality" activities that help to build the parent-child relationship. Tuning into a television program with your child often means tuning out each other. The television program provides entertainment while you and your child absorb what is being presented. Attending a ball game together is not a quality-time activity either, because others are still providing the entertainment. Ball games provide only limited interaction between you and your child.

3. *Make family time quality time.* Make a ritual out of those precious times when your family is together. Having your child help you with dinner can include a sharing time during which daily events and achievements are discussed. If watching television is the only thing that your family can do together, then turn it into an educational experience by discussing the plot and characters. Ask your child how he or she might respond if placed in the situation portrayed in the television program. You might ask questions like:

   - "What would you do if you were in that situation?"
   - "Do you know anyone like that (character)?"
   - "Would you like to live next to that person?"
   - "Who is really the good guy in this show?"

   One word of warning. It is best not to discuss problems during quality family times, since these times should be kept pleasant. Problems should be discussed at a separate time in a quiet and comfortable setting.

4. *Build quality time into transportation time.* Do you sacrifice part of your in-home time to provide your child with chances to spend time with

friends in sports and club activities? If so, your family is being short-changed. You can make the best of ordinary routines. Make the car ride to and from after-school activities count by playing games and talking to your child. If you have a young school-age child, play games that involve counting the number of yellow, blue, or green objects (houses, cars) between destinations. Songs and jokes are other ways to interact with your child. If you have an older school-age child, the car ride is an ideal time to have heart-to-heart talks about peer or school problems. The car ride home from an activity provides the perfect opportunity for you to praise your child and to provide encouragement by using such statements as:

- "I am really proud of the way you handled that argument on the ball field today."
- "Your art work is getting better and better."
- "Even though your team lost, I think you are a winner. You did an excellent job today."

The car ride can also become an educational experience, providing you with an opportunity to teach your child about such safety practices as buckling up, driving defensively, and avoiding discussions that detract the driver from the flow of traffic. Pointing out and discussing the role of the different community services that you pass (hospital, health department, fire station, mental health center) make those emergency telephone numbers on the refrigerator door come alive. Discussing the activities that are carried out within those community services also helps your child learn more about the assistance he or she can count on when at home alone. Get your child involved in learning about the different sites you pass in your car. Ask such questions as:

- "What takes place there?"
- "When would you call the people who work in that building?"
- "How would you contact the people in that building if you needed their help?"

5. *Choose quality activities that you and your child enjoy.* Do not take part in an activity just because you feel you owe it to your child for the time that he or she spends alone. Such behavior sends the message

that you are apologizing for your work and the financial rewards it brings to the family. Children sense when things are done out of obligation rather than desire. These types of messages can backfire and build resentments from children. The best approach is to talk with your child about the things you both enjoy and can do together. It is much more important that you be yourself during quality-time activities than to second guess your child's expectations.

6. *Use relaxation time as quality time.* It is not a crime for working parents to be tired. And there is no rule that quality time has to involve action-packed activities. Many relaxing, slow-paced activities are available that can turn your relaxation time into quality time. Some children enjoy snuggling up with Mom or Dad to read a story or listen to music. Others enjoy relaxing beside a wading pool or in a hammock. If you are the adventurous type, you might suggest that your child practice his or her bandage-wrapping or make-up skills while you lie quietly awake.

7. *Use housework time as family time.* One of the most common concerns of working parents is that they may be demanding too much work from their children. In fact, giving your child some household responsibility is a good idea. Household chores help to structure your child's after-school time, while instilling a sense of family commitment and responsibility. Just remember to make sure the household chores are safe, fit your child's age, and allow your child free time to follow personal interests.

Try tackling household chores as a family project. Negotiate with your family to designate one night a week as "house-cleaning night." Make this night interesting. Put a list of household chores into a hat (cleaning bathroom, vacuuming, cleaning the litter box, folding laundry, dusting). Let each family member draw a household chore. Another idea is to let each family member briefly make an argument for why she or he would be the best person to carry out a certain household chore. Then take a vote to determine who should be assigned the different household chores.

Don't stop there. Make the family work-night fun by singing during your work, playing music, talking to one another, helping others out with a difficult chore, and ordering out for a pizza as a special treat. At all costs, try to avoid the "couch-potato" syndrome.

8. *Make quality-time educational time.* We have already mentioned some of the ways you can teach your child safety practices and responsibility through quality time activities. You may prefer an even more concentrated educational approach by taking on a parent-child project. Consider the following educational activities.

- Make a scrapbook of your family or town history.
- Trace the best route for your summer vacation.
- Create new family recipes.
- Prepare family meals together.
- Use mealtime to discuss the day's events or upcoming events.
- Make a family garden.
- Design clothing, housing, and cars for the year 2010.
- Write songs or poetry.
- Make puppets or models.
- Involve your child in the family budget.
- Design family Christmas cards.
- Write letters of support or protest to government officials. Encourage your child to express his or her own opinions.
- Take nature walks to collect leaves, feathers, etc.
- Landscape the yard.

9. *Make quality time realistic.* Keep quality time activities realistic to your family's lifestyle. Take note of your abilities and interests as well as those of your family members. Consider your daily schedule and that of your family. Don't be too ambitious. Deciding upon a new ''family exercise'' program is unrealistic if your spouse hates to sweat. Beginning a family photography club is unrealistic too, unless you have the space and money to purchase and set up a photography lab. Remodeling the bathroom is a good idea, but it may not match the abilities of your young child. It also takes time to remodel a bathroom; overlooking that point could turn a one-week activity into a one-year project.

   Ask yourself the following questions before deciding upon a family activity:

- Will everyone in my family enjoy this activity?
- Will everyone in my family be able to take part in this activity?
- How much will this activity cost?
- How long will it take to complete this activity?
- How much space is needed for this activity?

10. *Record quality time.* Keep your camera loaded to record whatever quality activities you undertake. The snapshots will be a source of great pride in the years ahead.

Planned Discipline

You have no choice but to depend upon your child to follow family rules and to behave properly. Good behavior does not just automatically happen when you walk out the door. Instead, you must plan for the types of behavior you want your child to have. We recommend that you use "planned discipline." Parents who use planned discipline instill, *not demand,* responsible behaviors from their children. This takes place as parents and children talk to each other and work through problems in the following ways.

1. *Show your child you care.* Showing you care about your child builds a foundation of mutual trust and respect—both of which are essential to planned discipline. Without trust and respect there is no common ground for negotiation or agreement on rules. And there is no assurance that your child will follow house rules. We have already covered the most important way for you to show your child that you care— quality time.

2. *Negotiate rules.* Share responsibility for a safer home-alone arrangement by negotiating rules of behavior and household duties. Don't be afraid to negotiate. Negotiation does not mean giving in to your child—far from it. Negotiation sends a clear message that you trust and have faith in your mutual ability to reach a fair decision about in-home rules. Willingness to negotiate reflects positively upon your self-confidence as a parent, and your child is more likely to respect you for the consideration you show for his or her feelings and intelligence.

Begin by making separate lists of the behaviors, in-home chores, and activities that are important for safe home-alone arrangements. Compare lists and negotiate which items should be dropped, modified, or added. Then get down to the details. Develop a parent-child contract. The contract includes a detailed list of rules to be followed when your child is at home alone, the household chores your child agrees to perform, and the logical consequences (see item four below) that follow violation of the rules and responsibilities. Once you and your child reach agreement, sign and date the contract.

Negotiating rules of behavior is an effective way to ensure that rules and responsibilities in the contract are followed. Your child is more likely to accept and abide by rules that he or she has had a part in making. Signing and posting the contract make the rules more visible and add a sense of legality to the contract.

3. *Teach your child to think independently.* The in-home safety of your home-alone child requires that he or she be able to think clearly and rationally when faced with a decision. You can help your child develop these skills by promoting independent thinking. In contrast, demanding blind obedience prevents your child from thinking through situations. As a result, your child ignores those situations for which you have failed to deliver specific instruction, or, worse yet, panics when faced with a dilemma.

We recognize that teaching your child to think independently can be threatening. It is helpful to keep in mind that teaching independent thinking does not mean you are encouraging your child to challenge your authority. Instead, it means you are nurturing the child's ability to examine many approaches, exploring the reasoning behind those approaches, and making decisions about which one works best for different situations. This is the type of independent thinking your child must develop to remain safe in a home-alone arrangement, since even the information given in a ''survival skills'' class may not always be relevant to every child's home situation.

4. *Use logical consequences.* We live in a society with rules, and those who break rules must learn to face consequences. You can teach your child about rules and responsible behavior through the use of logical consequences.

Logical consequences refer to the realistic consequences that follow when a child knowingly breaks a rule. For example, a logical consequence might be that your child must finish assigned chores before watching television that evening. A child who breaks a lamp as a result of roughhousing might be responsible for replacing it out of an allowance or through in-kind payment by performing additional household duties.

Logical consequences should be used in a matter-of-fact way. This means calmly discussing with your child the seriousness of the rule that has been broken and deciding upon a consequence that realistically fits the "crime." Then make sure the resulting consequence is carried out. A follow-up discussion should be held to consider any disagreements that your child might have with the broken rule. For example, does your child think that the rule is important? Does your child think the rule contradicts another rule? It is always helpful to end your discussion by brainstorming how the rule might be changed to make it more fair to your child and/or to think of ways by which your child might go about following the rule in the future. You and your child could choose to make logical consequences a formal affair by developing a parent-child contract like that described earlier.

5. *Have realistic expectations of your child.* Evaluate your child's physical, mental, and social-emotional skills using the information given in chapters 2, 3, and 4. Consider how your expectations fit your child's level of development. Are you demanding too much? When Kathleen matched the responsibilities of her home-alone arrangement to the abilities of her son, she realized he had fewer problems. In contrast, Beth took a strong-arm approach. She forced her daughter to follow rules and assume duties beyond her abilities. These burdens led to in-home stress and ultimately failure.

6. *Provide praise.* Praise is the best way to ensure responsible behavior while your child is at home alone. Your praise need not be elaborate. A simple "thank you" can go a long way in motivating children to continue following an after-school schedule. Even better, supply your child with more information. For example, you may say something like:

> John, I want you to know that I am very proud of your behavior. Your willingness to finish homework and begin dinner gives us more family time at night. Thanks!

Make a conscious effort to say something positive to your child each day. Make a habit of giving praise during dinner or some other family time when everyone, or hopefully almost everyone, is present. It is easier to get in a habit of providing praise if you do it at the same time each day. Providing praise in front of others makes it more powerful.

7. *Engage your child in problem-solving.* Making a home-alone arrangement work means rechecking in-home rules and schedules on a regular basis. In some cases, a problem may arise that seems to have no solution. When this occurs, teach your child problem-solving skills as shown in the steps that follow:

   a. *State the problem in observable terms.* Make the problem-statement as observable and specific as possible. The statement, "Susan, your mom and I are not happy with your afternoon snack" is not specific enough. Are Susan's parents unhappy with the choice of a snack, the time it is eaten, or the quantity that is eaten? A more specific statement might be, "Susan, your mom and I are unhappy that you have chosen to eat cookies instead of the fruit which we agreed for you to eat." Susan now knows that her parents are unhappy with both her choice of an afternoon snack and with her decision to violate a family agreement.

   b. *Note the reason for your concern.* Susan's parents might explain, "Your mom and I feel that eating cookies is not a healthy practice and that there are more nutritious snacks available to you."

   c. *Generate multiple solutions.* Begin by stating the outcome that you would like to see. For example, Susan's parents might say, "We would like you to eat one of the snacks that we have all agreed to, like a peanut butter sandwich or fruit." Then open up the discussion. Susan's parents might say, "How do you feel about that?" Susan gets to express her views and offer an alternative solution. As a brainstorming session, this step welcomes all viewpoints and solutions.

   d. *Discuss the pros and cons of each solution.* It is helpful to list on a large sheet of paper all the solutions offered. Then follow up by comparing the advantages and disadvantages of each solution.

   e. *Identify one solution to try.* Ideally, you should end up with one solution to try. If, however, two or three solutions are identified, then the family will need to vote, ask for the opinion of someone else (a neighbor or friend), or use some other means (such as the flip of a coin) to decide upon one choice to try first.

f. *Develop a plan of action.* The details of the identified solution are planned next. The plan should include how, who, and when the steps of the plan will be carried out. In Susan's case, the plan of action may look something like this:

> *Solution:* To develop a new list of afternoon snacks.
>
> *How/Who:*
> - Visit the county home economist (Mom)
> - Visit the after-school program (Susan)
> - Look through nutrition books at the library (Dad)
>
> *Completion Date:* Thursday.

g. *Evaluate.* Set up a time to meet, evaluate, and plan for the next step. Susan and her parents, for instance, might decide to set aside some time the next evening to try out some of the recipes that are collected. Or they may modify their solution by contacting other resources, consider their second-choice solution, or identify a completely new solution by going back to step c.

Family Life and School-Age Children: Making It Work

Identification of a "strong family" was, until recently, a fairly easy job. Throughout time, the mark of a strong family was that it: (a) worked hard and "brought home the bacon"; (b) protected its members from hostile forces; (c) passed on religious values to its children; (d) educated its children; and (e) gave its members a certain status within society as defined by the wealth and/or occupation of family members. Times have changed rapidly during the past few decades; so, too, have families. Nowadays, it is much more difficult to use traditional indicators to define strong families. How often have you asked yourself the following questions?

- "Where did my paycheck go?"
- "How can I protect my child from drugs?"
- "How did my child develop that idea?"

- "Why don't I understand my child's homework assignments?"
- "How can I best prepare my child for a good job in the next century?"

These are difficult questions to answer. They reflect the trouble that parents like you have in meeting the traditional criteria of a "strong family." Are there any strong families out there? If so, what are their characteristics?

Most would agree that it takes hard work to build and maintain a strong family today. With this in mind, family scientists have changed the way they look at families. Instead of looking at how to "fix" families who are not living up to past standards, they look at families who thrive in modern society. As a result, we now have a new function for families. This new function is described by some as *relational*. It is a label that is likely to characterize strong families well into the next century.

But what does *relational* really mean? Simply put, it means one of the primary functions of families today is to provide their members with the emotional (or relational) support needed to play and work in a demanding and sometimes cruel world.

It should not be too surprising to learn that some people question whether even emotional support characterizes families today. After all, parents with home-alone children often worry about the quality of the emotional support they provide their children. But, as mentioned before, it is not simply a matter of the amount of time that families spend together, it is the quality of that time. Family scholars have spent the past decade studying strong families to identify how they build and maintain supportive and quality relationships. The identified traits can help you build family strengths and cope with family stressors.

1. *Family communication.* Strong families have members who communicate honestly with one another by sharing their needs and feelings. You can build your family communication skills in the following ways:

   - Make sure your verbal and nonverbal messages match. That is, make sure that your body language and words send the same message. Which of the following examples contains the same verbal and nonverbal message?

MOM: "I hear what you are saying." (washes dishes)

MOM: "I hear what you are saying." (looking at son)

It's difficult to believe that Mom is really listening when she is washing dishes. In fact, she is sending mixed messages, one of listening and the other of not listening. In addition to looking at your child, some other ways to nonverbally communicate that you are listening include putting aside your work, nodding your head to indicate that you understand what is being said, offering your child a cup of juice, and pulling your chair closer to your child.

Because we all communicate in different ways, it is important to check out what you think your child is saying by using such statements as, "Wow, it sounds like you are angry at me." "Let me be sure I understand; you're saying you are angry at me for not coming home on time."

- Ask for more information when you need it.
- Don't give your child a choice when there isn't one. Asking, "Beth what would you like to do this afternoon?" may result in a response that cannot be honored. In that case it is better to limit choices by asking, "Beth, would you like to go on the school field trip this afternoon or attend the library program?"
- Don't overcommunicate. Know when to stop talking and let your child share his or her feelings and thoughts.
- Understand good timing. Don't expect your child to be ready to communicate when he or she has had a bad day. Ask, "Is this a good time for us to talk about the after-school schedule?" Better yet, schedule a time to talk.

2. *Family support.* Strong families support one another during good and bad times. You can build your family support base in the following ways.

- Tell others in your family when you appreciate something they have done for you or someone else.
- Be sincere.
- Brag on your child's accomplishments.
- Tell your child how much you appreciate his or her unique traits.

- Avoid comparing your child to someone else.
- Encourage your child's interests and talents.
- Take the time each day to ask your child about his or her activities.
- Get away with your family for some "team time."
- Make sure that all family members have input on any family decision that will affect their lives.
- Admit your mistakes. Apologize when you discover you are wrong.

3. *Share responsibility.* Strong families have members who take an active role in family life. Some of the ways your family can share responsibility are:

- Assign each family member at least one household chore.
- Call a weekly family meeting to discuss problems or to make plans.
- Give your child a voice in helping plan the family budget. This will be a valuable lesson in money management.
- When a rule is violated, call the family together to discuss what happened, the consequences, and what can be done to correct the situation.

4. *A positive family outlook.* Strong families view life as a challenge, not a struggle. Problems are viewed as an opportunity to bring the family closer together, not break it apart. Changes in the family are viewed as normal, not as a sign of family break-up. You can help your child develop a positive outlook on life in the following ways.

- When something "bad" happens in your family bring everyone together to discuss what family lesson has been learned. Look for the "silver lining" in the unfortunate.
- Speak optimistically about the world. Look for something good to say about your life each day.
- Be trusting of others. Look for the positive in others, not the negative.
- Discuss how your family has handled a negative situation in the past and what positive things resulted.
- Plan ahead. Discuss with your family what challenges lie ahead.

Invite your child to predict what good things might lie ahead for the family as a result of the identified challenges.

5. *Individuality.* Strong families encourage each member to be an individual. They recognize and respect individual differences in values, music, art, food, and friends. You can encourage individuality in your family by following certain ground rules.

- Remember that each person has a right to speak. It is important that your child get to communicate freely and effectively. In short, children should be seen *and* heard.

- Remember that each person has a right to his or her beliefs. Respect your child's beliefs while playing a friendly game of challenge. Assume the role of "devil's advocate" by pointing out errors in your child's conclusions or beliefs. Encourage your child to argue his or her viewpoint by asking such questions as, "Why do you think that is true?" "Who else believes that?" "How did you come to that conclusion?" "What have you seen or read to support your idea?"

- Remember that each person has a right to have his or her remarks held in confidence. Your child's individuality should be nurtured within the family so that eventually it can sustain the challenges of the outside world. The personal information your child shares with you in confidence should remain a secret for this reason. Telling others may embarrass your child, who will in turn be less likely to confide in you in the future.

6. *Family play.* Strong families are protective of their play time. One way to plan for family play is to develop family rituals. Some suggestions:

- Plan special family meals.
- Plan family exercise time.
- Take weekly entertainment outings (movie, restaurant).
- Plan for Friday night grocery shopping.
- Make family Christmas gifts or cards.
- Take turns making Sunday morning breakfast.
- Write down family experiences.

- Spend family anniversaries at a special place.
- Identify a ''family member of the week'' who gets small secret gifts from other family members.
- Plant family trees, flowers, or vegetables.

7. _Family spirituality._ Strong families have deep spiritual beliefs upon which they base their lives. Spirituality need not be limited to religion. Your family may choose to build spiritual life around such themes as the golden rule, meditation, world peace, or environmental harmony.

8. _Family problem-solving._ Strong families do not ignore or run away from problems. Neither do they rely upon one approach to problem-solving. Strong families are assertive but flexible when dealing with problems. Here are some ways your family can prepare itself for problem-solving:

- Identify your resources. All families have resources, as reflected in their members' abilities and talents. The resources may be social (friends, church, civic club), emotional (family support, humor, empathy, communication), mental (foresight, ability to plan, logic, creativity), or financial (savings, checking account, bonds, house).
- Think of ways in which your family resources might help your family get through such problems as illness, job loss, or house loss.
- Again, plan ahead. Voice your concerns or frustrations. Plan a time for the family to pinpoint and work on a problem before it becomes a crisis.
- Seek help. Strong families are able to recognize when they need professional help, and they are willing to seek help. This may involve consultation with a financial planner, mental health counselor, nurse, minister, or school counselor.

Work Life: Keeping It Balanced

As we have already noted, one of the most significant trends in work during this century is the rise in the number of women in the labor force. Until the 1970s, most women who worked did so only temporarily. Beginning in the 1970s, more women moved into the labor force, mostly as a result of two factors: (1) sex roles changed during the 1960s, making it acceptable for women to express their talents outside the home; (2) what began as temporary employment for a down payment on a house or to help the family out of a financial crunch turned into a necessity.

While the movement of women into the labor force led to more sex role equality and helped relieve some family economic demands, problems continue to exist. Mothers, fathers, and children still deal with the personal strains brought on by increasing conflicts between work and family life.

Role Overload. Despite a hectic day at work, a parent must fulfill many household roles upon arriving home. You must be a nurse to a sick child, cook, disciplinarian, housekeeper, repairer, shopper, chaffeur, counselor, friend, lover, and so on. It is of little surprise that so many working parents like you find it difficult to spend time with children—there isn't any time available. This is especially true if you bear the dual responsibilities of household chores and wage earner.

Of course, working parents are not the only family members facing role overload. We have already noted how overwhelming are such adult-like roles assumed by home-alone children as cleaning, cooking, shopping, babysitting with younger siblings, and responding to emergencies.

Role Uncertainty. Because of the additional roles assumed by working parents and their home-alone children, it is sometimes difficult to say who has the most responsibility for some family roles. In one sense this is healthy; laundry, shopping, and meal preparation are easier when shared by family members. But in other cases shared roles between working parents and children need to be weighted. For example, a young child should know that a parent's directions override those of a supervising sibling in the afternoon. Otherwise, the younger child may be confused as to who is the primary (parents) versus secondary (older sibling) care giver. Clarification of child care roles helps the older sibling know where his or her authority to discipline a younger sibling stops.

Family Conflict. Who will do what, when, where, and how? Family conflict has become the norm for many working parents, and there is little reason to believe that things will soon change. Of the following conflicts, do any sound familiar?

- How will John get to his ball game by seven when Dad doesn't get home until seven-thirty and Mom must be at a PTA meeting by six-thirty?
- Who will prepare dinner in the single-parent home when Jane, an eight-year-old home-alone child, has been prohibited from cooking and her mother must work overtime?
- When will the family be able to take that long weekend vacation together when Mom works on Saturdays, Julie's swimming class is on Sunday, and Dad must be at the office early on Monday morning to work on a special project?

Social Support. One of the most frequent complaints we hear from parents is that they and their home-alone children are prisoners to their work or prisoners of their home. Parents complain that their social lives revolve around work and that they play golf or attend parties only with their work colleagues. Of course, all they talk about is work! Home-alone children complain that they are confined to a type of prison cell, since they are not allowed to go outside to play with friends and friends are not allowed into the house.

Job Burnout. We all know that workers who devote too much time to their jobs for too long a period eventually burn out. The term "workaholic" fits these individuals, since work seems to be an addiction from which they cannot escape. Unfortunately, burning out often affects family members as much as the worker. In some families the anger, depression, and confusion felt by the burned-out worker worry family members and place everyone under stress. In other cases, the emotional strain of burnout leads to family fights. And in still other families, the burned-out worker may feel abandoned when family members show little sympathy for what they believe is a just reward for overemphasizing work at the expense of the family.

Not all burnout is caused by workaholism. For some, work is not so much an addiction as it is a problem with life management skills. Some parents simply do not know when or how to let employers know when work demands are disrupting family life. The following suggestions can help you keep your work role in the proper perspective and give you more time to be with your family.

1. *Do not feel guilty about working.* Take pride in your willingness and ability to provide for your family; don't apologize. Your child is less likely to feel resentment toward the time you spend away from home if you have a positive attitude toward work. Talk about your job duties and their contribution to society. If possible, take your child to visit your workplace.

2. *Set life priorities.* To put your life in perspective, make a list of life priorities. Some things to consider include the importance of work, family, house, savings, entertainment, and your child's education. The ranking will not be easy, but try. It is helpful to first consider the values by which you live your life. Tuck your list of priorities in a secret place. Use it in two ways: (a) to periodically examine your life; (b) as a guide in resolving life decisions.

3. *Life goals.* Follow up your list of priorities by developing a list of life goals. This list is to keep your priorities in order. For example, if you rank your family as the top priority in your life, then spend most of your time developing goals related to building family strengths (see box 5–3).

4. *Leave work at the office.* This is not always easy to do. Paperwork must sometimes be brought home to meet a deadline. Job pressures sometimes overlap and affect home responsibilities. But there are ways to reduce that overlap. Keep track of the time you spend in job-related activities during work hours. You may find ways to spend more time "on task" by reducing the amount of time spent in socializing, daydreaming, taking breaks, or eating lunch. If office-related activities that detract from your work are optional, consider skipping some of them and remaining at your work station. Other ideas that can help you work more efficiently include:

• beginning work earlier
• organizing your work site
• examining the efficiency of your weekly schedule
• making lists of things to accomplish during a given day

Box 5–3   LIFE PRIORITIES AND GOALS

List your life priorities.	*List the life goals by which you plan to keep your life priorities in order.*
Life Priority #1	**Goals**
You should have the most goals for your #1 life priority.	
Life Priority #2	**Goals**
You should have fewer goals for your #2 life priority.	
Life Priority #3	**Goals**
You should have the fewest goals for your #3 life priority.	

- learning shorthand
- avoiding making difficult decisions alone
- returning calls in groups
- dictating instead of writing
- sending an assistant or aide to represent you at low-level meetings
- preparing your lunch at home instead of eating out
- eliminating office clutter

5. *Delegate.* Give up the old saying, "If you want something done right, do it yourself." Instead, delegate responsibility to colleagues, assistants, and secretaries.

6. *Plan ahead.* If you know a big project is due by a certain date, begin early to put the resource pieces into place. As the deadline approaches, it will be easier to make more efficient use of your time and energy by bringing the pieces together.

7. *Just say no.* Learning to be assertive about our rights is perhaps one of the most difficult tasks that we undertake in our work lives. Remember that you do not have to honor every request made of you. It is appropriate to indirectly say "no" by letting your employer know that while you appreciate the opportunity, it would interfere with the time you plan to be with your family. Parents who do not learn to say "no" to extra job duties often find themselves growing further and further apart from their families.

8. *Network outside of work.* Join a social club or civic group that does not include work colleagues. This outside link to new friends can stimulate and expand your own interests and talents beyond your daily work role. Consider the following options:

   - aerobic class
   - tennis or golf lessons
   - art class
   - church committee
   - cooking class
   - reading club
   - gardening club
   - running club
   - photography club

9. *Explore new ways to balance work and family demands.* Employers are beginning to experiment with ways to restructure the work responsibilities of their employees as a means of balancing demands of home and workplace. Here are some possibilities you and your colleagues might want to explore further with your employer:

   - *Flextime* allows you to complete a fixed number of hours a week according to your own schedule. One word of warning—family scientists have found that families who benefit the most from flextime are those without children.

- *Role cycling* involves parents' planning their lives so that personal, work, and family demands do not coincide. While a good idea, parents often find it difficult to follow through on this approach. For example, a young mother may find it hard to tell her employer, "I'm sorry, but I must turn down the promotion and pay raise because the work responsibilities do not fit with my family plan." On the other hand, some parents do seem able to forego job opportunities or delay beginning their family to keep their lives manageable. Many factors are part of successful role cycling, including careful and detailed long-term planning, a clear understanding and commitment between parents of their values and priorities, and, to some degree, luck.

- *Job sharing* involves two people sharing one full-time job by arranging their work duties and schedules to meet the needs of employers. One major drawback to this approach is that employers often resist paying benefits for two individuals who are filling only one job position.

- *Part-time employment* is an established alternative that working parents sometimes overlook. Take a close look at your family's financial needs in determining the amount of income on which you and your family can live. Consider your life priorities. You may decide that part-time work may be the ticket to providing your family with sufficient income so that one parent is able to be at home with the children during nonschool hours.

- *Flexplace* allows workers to perform their work duties at home. This arrangement is likely to become increasingly popular in the future as more computer links are made between offices and homes. Employers also like this approach because it reduces the cost of rental office space.

By now you have identified some ways to balance your work and family life. We would like to provide one more piece of information aimed specifically at you, the working parent.

Human development specialists with the Cooperative Extension Service have used Albert Ellis and Robert Harper's guide to rational living to address the potential effect that mental messages can have on your ability to keep your life in balance. Completing the following scale will tell you about your "balanced" mental messages.

Box 5-4 EXAMINING MENTAL MESSAGES

Ask yourself how strongly your Internal Messages *and* Outward Behaviors *reflect the following statements. Then write in the appropriate number: 1 = Strongly disagree; 2 = Disagree; 3 = Agree; 4 = Strongly agree.*

_____ 1. "I want to be loved by everyone."

_____ 2. "I must be thoroughly competent in all tasks I undertake."

_____ 3. "Other people upset me."

_____ 4. "My unhappiness is usually caused by events and people over which I have no control."

_____ 5. "I am responsible for my family's happiness."

_____ 6. "I avoid problems, hoping they will go away."

_____ 7. "I can't help the way I am."

_____ 8. "My way is the best way."

_____ 9. "Things have to be perfect for me to be happy."

_____ 10. "My destiny is set."

TOTAL _____ SCORE	*Add the numbers in the blanks. Put your total score in the space to the left.*

Interpretation of Box 5–4: This scale can serve as a guide to help you think about what effect your mental messages have upon your ability to keep your life circle (child, family, work) balanced.

One – ten	It is *highly likely* that your mental messages will lead to a *balanced* view of life.
Eleven – twenty	It is *probable* that your mental messages will lead to a *balanced* view of life.
Twenty-one – thirty	It is *probable* that your mental messages will lead to an *unbalanced* view of life.
Thirty-one – forty	It is *highly likely* that your mental messages will lead to an *unbalanced* view of life.

It is useless to know how "unbalanced" your mental messages are unless there is some way to change them. The information that follows can help you to do just that. For every *unbalanced message* we have supplied a *balanced message*. Practice substituting a balanced message every time you catch yourself using an unbalanced one. After a period of dedicated practice you should begin to see a difference in your ability to keep your life circle balanced.

Unbalanced Messages	Balanced Messages
"I want to be loved by everyone."	"It would be nice to be loved by everyone, but that is unrealistic. My worth doesn't depend on everyone's liking me."
"I must be thoroughly competent in all tasks I undertake."	"Trying to be outstanding even in one task is very difficult. Achievements do not determine my worth."
"Other people upset me."	"I let other people upset me."
"My unhappiness is usually caused by events and people over which I have no control."	"I can control many things that happen to me by asserting my needs and opinions."
"I am responsible for the happiness of my family."	"I am responsible for my behavior and happiness while others are responsible for their behavior and happiness."
"I avoid problems, hoping they will go away."	"Facing problems early on results in less hassle and is more rewarding."
"I can't help the way I am."	"It is up to me to change the things I can that get me in trouble."
"My way is the best way."	"There are many ways to get something done. Mine is only one way. I am willing to listen and negotiate."
"Things have to be perfect for me to be happy."	"Life is uncertain, and people, myself included, are not perfect."
"My destiny is set."	"Anything is possible. I take responsibility for my future."

6

What Can You Do
When Home-Alone Care
Is Not Working?

I F you have followed the steps we have outlined so far, chances are
your family has successful home-alone care. Most households find a
match between the needs of children and adults and their home-alone
arrangements. When self-care works, children feel reassured and successful and parents take pride in seeing them grow up with confidence and
self-reliance. But being home is overwhelming and disturbing for some
school-age youngsters who feel threatened and fearful. No amount of
coaching or preparation seems to fill the gap between security and
doubt. Although home-alone care can be worked out most of the time,
there are times when parents must look elsewhere for help. Today more
than one-half of single and married mothers of school-age children
scramble to find suitable care for their youngsters while they work. If
you feel your child is not adjusting to his or her home-alone arrangement, there are other steps you can take.

Alternatives to Being Home Alone

June Kirby of Live Oak, Fla., tried several after-school arrangements
before settling on her current one. Her fourteen-year-old son can take
care of himself, but leaving eight-year-old daughter Nickey in his charge
did not work out because of their constant squabbling.

June tried picking Nickey up after school and taking her to a day care center, then racing back to her job as a bank officer. That arrangement ended when Nickey complained that the owner made her change the younger children's diapers and give them their snacks.

"Her friends call her 'baby'," complained June. "Still, she was too young to stay home alone. And unfortunately, no school-age programs are available in this area."

Having exhausted all other possibilities, June now picks up her daughter after school and takes her back to the bank where she works. Nickey does not mind too much. "It's sort of fun," she says with a grin. "I go back and draw and help my mom put things in envelopes, but I wish I could go home and play with my friends." If you find yourself in a pinch like June Kirby, you have a number of other possibilities available to you.

June is fortunate. Many employers don't allow parents to bring children to work with them. More and more parents are finding that school-age child care is the answer. School-age child care is designed to provide care before and after school, on snow days, and during school vacations and holidays for elementary school youngsters while their parents work. Typical programs blend quality child care, recreation, and academic enrichment. Many agencies sponsor school-age child care, depending on the locale.

Emotional Benefits of After-School Programs

Kathleen Wilmore of Charlotte, N.C., worried about adequate after-school care when her five-year-old son began kindergarten. William was lucky enough to attend one of the hundreds of elementary schools in this country that offer extended-day programs. Such programs are designed to provide before- and after-school care in kindergarten through fifth grade for children of single and working parents.

"William loves the program because there's so much to do, and he can play with his friends!" says Kathleen. "I like it because I know he's learning and having fun in a well-supervised program. There are benefits for me too. He stays at school, which eliminates any transportation hassles, and I'm more productive in my work because my mind is at ease."

The continuity and dependability of after-school care is one of its major benefits to children and parents. Unlike more informal arrangements—such as babysitters who become ill at the last minute or neighbors who are called away unexpectedly—after-school programs provide a more stable structure, eliminating undue fear and anxiety for the whole family. The program is always there, and the children can count on it. Security in the program also permits better work productivity of parents: they don't interrupt their work schedules to worry about their children. After-school programs replace the loneliness, boredom, and fear of going home to an empty house. The safe and stimulating programs offer alternatives where play and social interaction are high priorities.

Educational Benefits of After-School Programs

Studies have shown that extended day programs offer distinct educational advantages for children, even though the curricula have a non-academic, enrichment emphasis. The Phillips Magnet Extended Day School in Raleigh, N.C., was the first licensed day care elementary school in the southeast. Open from 7:00 A.M. to 6:00 P.M., the enrichment program expands the curriculum offered during the school day. Former principal Mary Mayesky compared scores on statewide reading and math tests for two years of children enrolled in the extended-day program and those not enrolled. Children participating in the program had much higher scores in math and reading than nonparticipating children. Differences in achievement scores were attributed to the program, which included high-interest activities, qualified staff, low adult-child ratio, and a nonthreatening setting.

Another study by Barbara Entwisle reported similar results in a center-based after-school program in Baltimore, Md. Children participating in the program had higher gains in reading and math over a six-month period compared to a group of children not enrolled in the program. These improvements held true despite the fact that the curriculum was not specifically created to stimulate achievement. Self-esteem also improved among boys and girls in the program.

Although these two studies suggest clear advantages to after-school programs in public schools, other studies find that positive benefits for children depend upon the program's curriculum. Deborah Vandell, at the University of Texas, compared children in after-school programs in day care centers with children in self-care. Day care programs were mainly for preschoolers and did not provide organized, after-school activities for school-age children. Vandell found that teachers rated day care school-age children more poorly on work and study habits. Playmates also rated day care children more negatively than home-alone kids. Day care children may have been rated inferior to home-alone children because they disliked the program and the inappropriate activities may have been fostering inadequate development. Vandell found that the third graders complained about going to the after-school programs because they were "for babies."

Closely investigate any after-school program before enrolling your child. Many children we talked to complained of after-school day care programs for preschoolers. Eight-year-old Michael, for example, said, "I used to go to Sandbox Nursery where my little sister goes, but I stopped going last year in the second grade. The first two or three weeks, it kind of got boring and stuff at the day care center. It wasn't much fun. I just didn't want to go back. In day care if it gets too cold, they won't take you outside to play. I didn't feel very good because there wasn't much freedom. I wanted to be home instead of in a day care center because I can play with my friends. I just didn't want to go back. I told my mom about it, and she said we'll start letting you go home and see if you do okay."

A Menu of After-School Programs

If you have a child at home alone and it's not working, or if your child is in some arrangement after school with which you are dissatisfied, check into the possibility of an after-school program in your area. There are many types of after-school programs, some better than others. Never enroll your child in one without first having made a personal visit to the facility. Some regions have extended-day programs in elementary schools. Other areas have programs sponsored by departments of parks and recreation, churches, or Y's. Many private day care centers also provide before- and after-school care. Some parts of the country are fortunate enough to have several or all of these choices available, while others have few or none. The following list offers you a menu of after-school programs from which to select.

Private Day Care Centers

Many commercial day care centers have expanded their programs to include before- and after-school care for children. The quality of after-school day care programs depends on state and local licensing requirements and the different child care philosophies of the operators. Investigate a day care center before enrolling your child. Look for staff training, hours of operation, cost factors, safety precautions, transportation services to and from school, and staff-child ratio (one adult for every ten children).

One of the most common complaints about day care programs is that school-age children become quickly bored and unhappy with curricula that emphasize preschool care. Children like Nickey complain that these programs are too babyish. Others like Michael get bored when programs don't meet their needs and interests. Once you have checked on the basics, make sure that separate groups exist for older and younger children. Make sure the curriculum involves the children in the life of the community and emphasizes recreational and enrichment activities and does not overemphasize academics. A chief advantage of day care after school is that it provides services during nonschool days, such as school holidays and the summer months, when other after-school programs are closed.

Family Day Care Homes

For some parents the homes of neighbors, relatives, and friends represent a valuable source of after-school care. Licensing and registration requirements for family day care homes are different from day care centers. In some instances, family day care homes register with state or local offices, but no licensing is required. Some communities have a private agency that brings together a network of family day care homes to offer quality after-school care. The agency serves as a clearinghouse for parents seeking child care in a home setting. An advantage of family after-school care is that your child can stay in a homey atmosphere rather than an institutional one and the numbers of children are much smaller. A disadvantage is that care is usually directed at preschoolers which raises the boredom and babyish factors.

Recreation Service Agencies

Recreational youth service agencies such as the YWCA, YMCA, Scouts, and parks and recreation organizations offer exceptional after-school programs in many areas of the country. The recreational and enrichment curricula offered by these agencies are so attractive that getting children to attend these programs is rarely a problem. Activities include supervised free play and structured classes in crafts, cooking, water safety, and other skills. Most of these programs have staff trained to work with school-age youngsters and many offer their services not only after school, but also on weekends and summers.

Church-Sponsored After-School Care

Church-sponsored school-age child care programs are sometimes preferred by parents not only because they are safe but also because they provide a religious atmosphere that contributes to their child's spiritual growth. A distinct advantage of church-sponsored programs is that many support systems are already in place. Young adults, parents, and high school and college students serve as care providers. Parents often already know the staff well and feel confident in the quality of after-school experiences. Children feel secure in a familiar setting. Financial support is drawn from the congregation and from community fund drives. Many churches have buildings for conducting youth programs, and with some planning these buildings are made available for school-age child care.

Employer-Sponsored After-School Care

To cut down on the "three o'clock syndrome" more employers are participating in after-school care. Corporate after-school care, although less common than the other types, is cropping up as employers realize that it reduces absenteeism and employee turnover, as well as improves productivity. A survey of 211 companies showed that 40 percent of them provided on-site or near-site after-school care for employees' children. If you are lucky enough to work where you have such a service, your mind will be more at ease knowing your child is only a few steps away and that you can even visit on your break. You can build in quality time with your child while driving home from work in the afternoons. If you are job hunting, this may be one of the factors you look for in choosing an employer.

Public School Extended-Day Programs

The most common, affordable, and popular type of after-school programs are extended-day programs, housed in elementary schools. These programs operate before and after school, on teacher work days, and on bad-weather days. With an emphasis on enrichment, time is allotted for arts and crafts, homework, snacks, field trips, sports, and free play. Certified school teachers work in some programs, while high school students, volunteers, parents, and aides are employed in others. Funding for extended-day programs is based solely on parent fees. Some programs have a special scholarship fund for families who need financial support. Others provide after-school care in exchange for the parents' in-kind service to the program.

Steps in Selecting the Right Program for You

The first step in selecting an appropriate program is to find out what after-school care choices are in your area. Call your local child care referral agency or social services department and inquire. Check with your child's school about the existence of an extended-day program.

If you're fortunate enough to have several choices, visit the ones that sound the most appealing and observe for a day before enrolling your child. Regardless of the sponsor, good after-school child care should provide a safe and well supervised environment and should provide more than just babysitting or school work. Because children spend a greater portion of their day in educational settings, a quality after-school program should have an informal, relaxed atmosphere in which children can choose from a wide range of activities: arts and crafts, occasional field

---

Box 6–1 A CHECKLIST OF CHOICES

Private Day Care Center

- Offers before- and after-school care as a change from the academic setting the child has been in all day
- Operates during holidays and summer vacations
- Keeps emergency information on children
- Provides transportation in many cases
- Keeps siblings together
- Offers small group and leisure activities

Caution: The preschool curricula of many day care centers are not tailored for older school-age children. Poor regulations and licensing requirements do not guarantee trained staff or developmentally appropriate activities.

Family Day Care Home

- Provides a natural home setting in a relaxed atmosphere
- Serves children of all ages
- Offers small, personal groups
- Allows parents to contract for specific services
- Presents opportunities for one-to-one, adult-child relationships
- Provides infrequent turn over of caregiver

Caution: Monitoring of family home care by governmental agencies is difficult. Quality of care is determined solely by the skill of the caregiver.

Recreation Service Agency

- Practices flexible scheduling
- Promotes wide choice of activities and group games
- Uses facilities designed for recreation and leisure
- Employs well qualified, trained staff
- Provides age-integrated programs so that younger kids can rub elbows with and learn from older ones
- Uses volunteers and senior citizens
- Operates on holidays and during summer vacations

Church-Sponsored Program

- Provides a familiar setting for parent and child
- Keeps cost at a reasonable level
- Allows the extra benefit of spiritual growth for your child in the denomination of your choice

---

Box 6-1 A CHECKLIST OF CHOICES (Continued)

Employer-Sponsored Program

- Improves parent's job performance
- Allows child to be cared for near parent
- Increases amount of quality time spent with child through breaks and driving home in afternoons
- Eases parent's mind
- Maintains low cost level

School-Based Program

- Permits extended-day programs in the child's school setting
- Eliminates transportation problems
- Gears activities to children's interests
- Provides help with homework
- Employs well trained staff
- Provides familiar setting for children
- Facilitates personal attention with low adult-child ratios

Caution: Most school-based programs do not operate on holidays or during summer vacations.

---

trips, organized games, club memberships, homework time, music, films, reading, free time for children to pursue their favorite interests, and other recreational and enrichment activities. A lower adult-child ratio than is possible during the regular school day is also a plus for a high-quality program.

Cost for after-school care ranges widely, depending upon who offers the care. Where cost is a consideration, most programs offer a sliding-scale fee based on income adjusted for size of family. Ask about scholarships. Many after-school programs provide some free care in the form of scholarships for families that cannot afford the minimum costs.

One of the biggest problems parents have is knowing how to tell the difference between good after-school programs from bad ones. The checklist in box 6–2 will help you select and monitor a good program for your child.

Box 6–2 SELECTING AN AFTER-SCHOOL PROGRAM

_____ Is the program safe? Every precaution must be taken to insure protection from hazards to health and physical safety.

_____ Is the program closely supervised? Adequate teacher/pupil ratios should be maintained. Ideally, the ratio should be one teacher for every ten children to allow for child-centered activities.

_____ What ages of children are served? There are many choices: Kindergarten–third grade; first–sixth grade; and even first–ninth grade! Choose a program that gives attention to the age of your child.

_____ Do the teachers express a caring attitude toward the children?

_____ Are opportunities provided for in-service training of the staff?

_____ Does the program meet during the hours you need? Some programs offer only after-school care; others provide before- and after-school care. Also ask about holidays during the school year and whether the program is extended in the summer.

_____ Is the program accessible to your child? What provision is made for your child to get to the program after school? Programs have various policies such as personally providing transportation for school-age children, using public school buses, or organizing car pools. The best accessibility is offered when the program is either near the child's home, the child's school, or the parent's place of employment.

_____ Does the program encourage parent involvement? Even though parents using these programs have limited time for participation, provision should be made for regular communication with and input from all parents. Whenever possible, parents should be used as resource persons in the program.

_____ How long has the program been in operation? Longevity in the community often is an indication of program stability.

_____ Does the program have clearly defined purposes?

Perhaps even more important than parental preference in choosing school-age child care are criteria that deal with the developmental needs of children. A successful program will be responsive to the unique needs of the children who attend. The following checklist will help determine whether the needs of children are being taken into consideration.

(Box continued)

Box 6–2 SELECTING AN AFTER-SCHOOL PROGRAM (Continued)

_____ Is time provided for physical activity? Time should also be allowed for relaxation. Children who come from school need a time to wind down. They also need plenty of space for using energy constructively.

_____ Does the program encourage children to develop competence? Are there opportunities for them to achieve? A balanced program provides children ways to sense their value and their ability to contribute to the group. School-age child care should also provide a low-risk environment for the child to try new skills. These include academic as well as motor and social skills.

_____ Is there an emphasis on helping the child learn more about himself? The staff must be sensitive to the child's feelings about himself. A relaxed schedule that allows time for informal conversation with the staff and peers helps the child gain a sense of self-awareness.

_____ What encouragement is given to creative activities? Are there opportunities for involvement in art, drama, reading, and music? Children can find creative expression through sports and recreation, gardening, and games. Effective child care centers will strive continually to provide varied creative opportunities to keep programs interesting and attractive.

_____ Is there social interaction with peers and adults on the staff? Program activities are not as important to the child as are relationships with the staff and the peer group. Emphasis should be given to drawing out the positive relationships. Many times this will minimize negative behavior.

_____ Are there clearly defined expectations for children in the program? Do they know what is expected of them? Clear boundaries within which the children can function are critical. Rules about behavior should be explicitly stated. Children function productively, are more cooperative, and become more secure in an environment influenced by the love and care of teachers who set limits for safety and behavior.

_____ Does the program allow for meaningful participation? Activities and schedules must be conducive to the child's involvement in the program. This is true in the daily routine and in special projects. Many school-age programs offer mission- or service-oriented activities. A balanced program will offer a variety of activities for diverse interests.

Starting Your Own After-School Program

If you're faced with no choices or are dissatisfied with the programs you have found, you might want to begin a program of your own. To start some type of organized supervision for your child after school, your best bet is to link with other parents in your area. Your local Parent-Teacher Association (PTA) is a group already in place that you could work through. The National PTA has been instrumental in speaking out on good care for home-alone kids, and PTAs across the country play a key role in dealing with latchkey issues. A latchkey task force, in conjunction with the PTA, could advise principals in making school decisions and address the urgent needs of home-alone children and their families. Parents, teachers, administrators, and school counselors working cooperatively on a task force would provide common goals, bring multifaceted expertise to self-care issues, and improve communication. Projects might include developing policies for emergency and sick care or determining the need for before- and after-school care for school children.

Local PTAs can begin advocacy efforts by investigating choices for after-school care available in their areas. Calls to community child care referral agencies and social services departments, as well as inquiries about local child care options, are starting points. PTAs can inform parents of their findings at regular meetings or through special newsletters. Some PTAs publish brochures advising parents on what to look for in quality after-school programs. In some areas the next step is an informal talk with parents and school officials about the possibility of starting an extended-day program. A more formal needs assessment, however, is often essential to determine the need for after-school care. A sample needs assessment form is available from the National PTA (see chapter 7 for address).

Another way to determine your local needs is to plan a special self-care night at a PTA meeting. The film *Lord of the Locks* (see chapter 7 for ordering information) could be shown to stimulate questions, reactions, and discussion. Small groups can brainstorm ways of addressing school and community needs after the film. The groups then can share their proposed solutions in a large-group meeting where a master proposal is generated from small-group lists. The John Adams PTA and the North Brunswick Township Department of Human Services, through this approach, established a school-age child care program in their New Jersey community. The program attracts children by offering computer instruction, gymnastics, dramatics, arts and crafts, and cooking activities for forty-four children in kindergarten through sixth grades. The original staff included a program supervisor, four high school students, a senior citizen, and a college student.

Depending on the results of your needs assessment, your PTA also can explore the possibility of starting some type of after-school program or organized supervision that matches your school's needs. There are many kinds of supports you can start in your own community. Some parent groups have instituted extended day programs, neighborhood block mothers, after-school check-in programs, afternoon help lines, or concerted efforts between community agencies in operating before- and after-school centers.

Extended-Day Programs

If you do not have an extended-day program, talk with other parents and local officials about the possibility of starting one. One of the first public school systems to provide extended-day programs was the Arlington, Va., public school system. For more information contact: Extended-Day Program, Arlington Public Schools, 1426 North Quincy Street, Arlington, Va. 22207.

Parent-Run Programs

Many parent-run after-school child care programs have achieved roaring success in different parts of the country. The School-Age Child Care Project at Wellesley College can assist you in this regard. Information on how to start an after-school program and on other successful parent-run programs is available from the School-Age Child Care Project, Center for Research on Women, Wellesley College, Wellesley, Mass., 02181.

Check-in Programs

Some communities have check-in programs that creatively combine self-care with adult supervision. Designated block mothers serve as check points for older elementary and junior high children who wish to spend time in their own homes, visit friends, play outside in their neighborhoods, or attend special community events. This way children have more contact with neighborhood friends and parents have less difficulty with transportation. These programs offer indirect supervision where adults are available but children are given more responsibility for being on their own. Block parent programs take a number of forms.

In Fairfax Country, Va., the Reston Children's Center Senior Satellite Program sponsors a check-in program for older school-age children. Children are assigned to a trained neighborhood family day care provider who carries out a contract developed by the children, their parents, the Reston Center, and the providers. Each contract is different. Some children use their neighborhood provider's home as a check-in point before attending an after-school activity. Others spend most of their after-school time in the home of the provider. The Reston check-in program is a good example of a developmentally sound program that provides child care while recognizing the developmental needs of preadolescents.

Safety Haven programs, like the one in Charlotte, N.C., designate certain homes with identifiable logos in their windows as places where children can retreat in emergencies, such as when a stranger follows them home from school or when an accident requires medical attention. These homes have block mothers who oversee safe travel as children walk to and from school.

A somewhat different type of block parent arrangement is the Home Based Child Care Program in Orlando, Fla. Before- and after-school care is provided in the homes of certified, insured, and trained providers. Children are cared for within a safe, supervised home environment where they enjoy books and toys supplied through a resource library, do homework under adult supervision, and participate in youth programs and activities.

The Family Day Care Check-in Project in Fairfax provides a comprehensive package of materials for those interested in adapting the Family Day Care Check-in Project in their neighborhoods. The package contains step-by-step directions for starting up, administering, supervising, and evaluating your program. In addition to addressing such issues as licensing, zoning, and liability, the materials include a section on community outreach, describing methods of educating the community about the needs and problems of unsupervised young adolescents. Write The Fairfax County Office for Children, 11212 Waples Mill Road, Fairfax, Va., 22030.

Telephone Helplines

Helplines provide emotional support and information for home-alone children who are scared or who just need to talk with someone. Services include supplying information on how to handle minor problems and referral for circumstances that require special attention. Volunteers are trained to staff the telephones and work under the guidance of professional staff.

The best-known helpline is called PhoneFriend. The goals of Phone-Friend are to create a helping network to provide information and support for home-alone children after school hours, to help these kids help themselves, and to increase community awareness of the children's needs. Children call PhoneFriend for many reasons. The majority of calls come from eight- and nine-year-old children who say they just want to talk. Many others say they are bored, lonely, scared, or just curious about PhoneFriend.

PhoneFriend started out of State College, Pa., and is operated by two women's groups. Hours of operation are from 2:30 to 5:30 P.M. during school days and 9:00 A.M. to 5:30 P.M. on days when school is not in session because of teacher workdays or bad weather. Mothers or students with some background in the helping professions serve as volunteers. A PhoneFriend replication packet giving information and instruction on how to establish and operate a helpline for children is available from the following address: PhoneFriend, P.O. Box 735, State College, Pa., 16804.

Survival Training Programs

Numerous training programs have been developed to help unsupervised children handle more responsibility while parents work. Girl Scouts of America has published a survival skills booklet, *Safe and Sound at Home Alone;* Boy Scouts of America produced a manual, *Prepared for Today;* Camp Fire Inc. has written a program called *I Can Do It* for children between second and fourth grades; and the Kansas Committee for Pre-

vention of Child Abuse developed the *I'm in Charge* program for parents
and their home-alone children.

These programs teach children how to follow safety rules, respond
in emergencies, care for younger siblings, problem-solve, understand
their neighborhoods, and plan meals. Many have lessons for parents on
setting rules and developing communication skills that help with the
many headaches of home-alone arrangements. Addresses of these
organizations and their available survival programs can be found in the
next chapter.

Parents Taking Community Action

When home-alone arrangements don't work, it is not just a family
problem, it is a community problem. For those of you who are active
community leaders, there is a lot you can do in your community.

Publicity

The first step is to educate the community about the home-alone problem. Many people do not know what the phrase "latchkey child" or
"home-alone child" means. Writing letters to the local newspaper is
one way to educate the public and stimulate community action. Writing
radio public service announcements is another educational strategy.
Radio stations air public service spots, like the following one, free of
charge:

FOR IMMEDIATE NEWS RELEASE

Topic: Home-Alone Children

"Does your child arrive to an empty home after school? If so, you have
a home-alone child, sometimes called a "latchkey child." Home-alone
children care for themselves when not in school and while their parents
are at work. Communities from across our country are developing programs to protect these children. [Name of community] has no program
for its home-alone youth. If you are interested in working on this problem, please join [name of parent group]. Call [telephone number] for
more information."

Networking

Networking is the most efficient means to resolve the home-alone problem; individual parents can accomplish only so much. Parent groups have greater visibility and resources. The first step in forming a parent group is to develop a plan. Some parents will be interested only in public education. Others will want to establish informal block parent groups. Still others will want to serve as advocates and work with community agencies in developing school-age child care programs. Ask parents about their interests and get a consensus on the types of programs that are top priority.

Employers

Employers can help with the home-alone problem. Parents who know company policies and the personality traits of the employer are more effective in pursuading companies to develop ways of resolving the after-school problem. One possible solution is a three to three-fifteen break when employees can call home or visit their children at on-site after-school programs. Flextime, job sharing, and employer-sponsored programs are other ideas. Having a number of suggestions will help sell your ideas. Supply figures and charts to show how your suggestions will benefit the company. Point out the benefits of increased productivity, decreased absenteeism, and greater worker loyalty.

Churches

Churches can sponsor after-school programs ranging from simple discussion groups to elaborate activity centers. Churches can usually cut through red tape and recruit funds and staff to facilitate programs. In some instances the community is more likely to listen to clergy than a human service worker or politician.

Community Agencies

Many community agencies already have programs that address the concerns of parents with home-alone kids, but the programs may not be well coordinated. The fire department, police department, church, PTA, county extension office, parks and recreation departments, Y's, girls and boys clubs, and mental health offices have child development and child safety programs. These programs can be linked with some coordination. A local community center, school, or church can conduct a series of programs on the issues. Each community agency can develop a schedule of times and types of activities it offers. Parental coordination efforts can represent the beginning of program development. Communities sometimes need a demonstration of resources and capabilities before a commitment to programming is made. Publicizing the program helps convince community leaders that school-age child care is needed and realistic. By networking with community agencies, parent leaders can meet the difficult challenge of opening doors for home-alone children and their families. If you are a parent with a sense of commitment and vision who can see the overall picture of home, school, and community interlocking and working harmoniously, then you are the one who will ultimately find the greatest success in your efforts.

7

How Can You Bolster
Your Child's Home-Alone Care?
A Knapsack of Resources

T HIS section contains resources that can help you bolster your child's home-alone arrangement. It contains a reading list of books for you and your child. Reading other materials will help you get many different points of view. Your child's reading list will help him or her gain more confidence in being home alone. Magazines and newsletters are also listed. We have included the ones we believe will keep you abreast of changes and current thought about self-care and alternatives that are being established nationwide.

We also include names and addresses of organizations for those of you who are action takers in PTAs or who want to establish community programs. These organizations will mail you inexpensive replication packets with step-by-step instructions. There is a list of the best audiovisuals, which can be used at PTA or community meetings to show the scope of the need for more programs for home-alone kids. Films for children can be used in training programs on safety and care. Twenty-four fun ideas that we call Boredom Busters can be carried out by you and your child together in the evenings or by your child when home alone.

Books for Parents

After-School Activities

Baden Ruth; Genser, Andrea; Levine, James; and Seligson, Michelle. 1982. *School-age child care: An action manual.* Boston, Auburn House. A comprehensive guide on how to set up school-age child care programs. Information is given for parents on what they need to know.

Bergstrom, Joan. 1984. *School's out—now what? Creative choices for your child.* Berkeley, Calif.: Ten Speed Press. Presents ways for parents to provide practical help and guidance for their school-age children for afternoons, weekends, and vacations. Gives resources, checklists, and ideas for busy parents to use with their school-age children.

Blau, R.; Brady, E.; Bucher, I.; Hiteshaw, B.; Zavitkovsky, A.; and Zavitkovsky, D. 1977. *Activities for school-age child care.* Washington, D.C.: National Association for the Education of Young Children. Provides an array of ideas for the child care curriculum—from puppets to gardening—for children between three and seven years.

Forman, George; and Hill, Fleet. 1986. *Constructive play.* St. Paul, Minn.: Toys N' Things. Includes more than one hundred games designed from child development that allow children to design their own rules and play at their own pace.

Hendon, K.; Grace, J.; Adams, D.; and Strapp, A. 1977. *The after-school day care handbook: How to start an after-school program for school-age children.* Madison, Wis.: Community Coordinated Child Care 4-C in Dane County. Order from: 4C in Dane County, 3200 Monroe Street, Madison, Wis., 53711.

High/Scope Consultants. 1985. *Hands-on after-school day care activities for five- to nine-year-olds.* Ypsilanti, Mich.: High/Scope Press. A series of five books to help children generate their own projects and activities after school: *Learning through sewing and pattern design* (making and using patterns to create toys, puppets, and clothes); *Learning through construction* (building with wood); *Children as music makers* (writing and reading stories and plays, writing plans for activities); *Writing and reading* (writing and reading stories and plays, writing plans for activities); *Daily routine: Small group time* (one hundred child-tested activities in art, drama, sewing, construction, music, movement, math, writing, reading, classification, seriation, space, and time). Order from: High/Scope Press, 600 North River Street, Ypsilanti, Mich., 48198.

Oregson, Bob. 1986. *The incredible indoor games book.* St. Paul, Minn.: Toys N' Things. An unlimited resource for games and activities that require little preparation and are designed for children between the ages of six and sixteen.

Working Parents and Home-Alone Kids

Berg, Barbara. 1986. *The crisis of the working mother.* New York: Summit Books. Helps working moms resolve the conflict of splitting time between family and work.

Gorelick, Byrna. 1986. *The working parent's guide to child care.* St. Paul, Minn.: Toys N' Things. Covers the pros and cons of in-home care, family day care, and center care. Draws on latest research, important issues such as interviewing caregivers, evaluating settings, contracts, adjustment to day care, and costs.

Grollman, Earl; and Sweder, Gerri. 1986. *The working parent dilemma.* Boston: Beacon Press. More than a thousand kids of working parents were interviewed by the authors. Their creative tips to problems of having working parents comprise the book's content. Some of the children were kids in self-care and some were not. But their messages are interesting, clear, and worth hearing.

Long, Lynette; and Long, Thomas. 1983. *The handbook for latchkey children and their parents: A complete guide for latchkey kids and their working parents.* New York: Arbor House. Based on five hundred interviews, describes the positive and negative aspects of home-alone arrangements and projected consequences. Includes suggestions for parents and survival skills for children.

Rauch, Gay; and Schmitt, Gretchen. 1986. *Single parenting.* St. Paul, Minn.: Toys N' Things. Describes a course to help parents meet the demands of their special roles as single parents. Handouts, bibliographies, and exercises for participants make this a complete and easily adopted curriculum.

Robinson, Bryan; Rowland, Bobbie; and Coleman, Mick. 1986. *Latchkey kids: Unlocking doors for children and their families.* Lexington, Mass.: Lexington Books. Written primarily for parents and educators who want to take action in their communities through advocacy groups and setting up special supervised programs or hotlines for after-school home-alone children. A special chapter for parents tells what they can do at home.

Stress and Safety

Brenner, Avis. 1984. *Helping children cope with stress.* Lexington, Mass.: Lexington Books. Presents tips on how to relieve stress in children's lives so they can grow and develop in more healthy ways.

Elkind, David. 1981. *The hurried child.* Reading, Mass.: Addison-Wesley. Describes how society is pushing children to grow up before they are developmentally ready and offers insights, advice, and hope for solving these problems.

Elkind, David. 1984. *All grown up and no place to go.* Reading, Mass.: Addison-Wesley. A sequel to *The hurried child* that focuses on the problems youth face as a result of being hurried.

Hechinger, Grace. 1984. *How to raise a street-smart child: Complete parent's guide to safety on the street and at home.* New York: Facts on File Publications. Attempts to give children a sense of personal security and safety by teaching them to take reasonable precautions. Topics include safety in traffic, risks at home, sexual abuse, missing children, muggings, and gangs and bullies.

Kraizer, Sherryll. 1985. *The safe child book.* New York: Dell Publishers. Describes for parents a complete program on developing prevention of abduction and sexual abuse of children as well as safety training. The approach stresses that children can be taught to protect themselves without making them fearful. The author takes the point of view that children can make judgments, speak up for themselves, and play a major role in being responsible for their own well-being.

Saunders, Antoinette; and Remsberg, Bonnie. 1985. *The stress-proof child: A loving parent's guide.* New York: Holt, Rinehart, and Winston. Explores many ways parents can remove stress in their children's lives.

Toys N' Things. 1986. *Health, safety, and first aid.* St. Paul, Minn.: Toys N' Things. Covers emergency first aid procedures, accident prevention, children's illnesses, health practices, and helping children learn safety and good health habits.

Winn, Marie. 1985. *Children without childhood.* New York: Penguin Books. Shows how childhood is disappearing and how working parents must now take the role of preparation as well as protection of their children.

Parenting

Cherry, Claire. 1987. *Parents: Please don't sit on your child.* Belmont, Calif.: David Lake Publishers, 19 Davis Drive, Belmont, Calif., 94002. An excellent book for parents on how to discipline children positively. The author gives a magic list of twelve alternative control techniques that prevent inappropriate behaviors.

Einstein, Elizabeth. 1982. *The stepfamily: Living, loving, and learning.* New York: Macmillan. An excellent account by the author on what it's like to be a stepchild and later a stepparent herself.

Farel, Anita. 1982. *Early adolescence: What parents need to know.* Carrboro, N.C.: Center for Early Adolescence. An easy-to-read handbook for parents seeking to understand the rapid physical, emotional, intellectual, and social changes their ten- to fifteen-year-old children are experiencing.

Flake, Carol; Robinson, Bryan; and Skeen, Patsy. 1983. *Child development and relationships.* New York: Random House. Provides a comprehensive coverage of growth and development from conception to adolescence. Special chapters are included on the school-age child's physical, cognitive, and social-emotional development.

Robinson, Bryan. 1989. *Work addiction.* Pompano Beach, Fla.: Health Communications. Provides help for parents who seek to balance their lives between family, work, and personal time. Also shows how pressure, stress, and family dysfunction in early childhood can lead to work addiction in adulthood.

Books for Home-Alone Kids

A new crop of books has been written especially for school-age kids. Some of these books emphasize the joys and problems of working parents from the child's point of view. Some explain to children why their parents must work and help ease the confusion and fears that occasionally accompany home-alone care. Other books furnish safety tips and constructive ways of occupying time while children are home alone. These resources can serve as a basis for starting a library for reading enjoyment at home or a lending library as a PTA project at school.

Alda, Arlene. 1982. *Sonya's mommy works.* New York: Simon and Schuster.

Bauer, Caroline. 1985. *My mom travels a lot.* New York: Penguin.

Blaine, Marge. 1980. *The terrible thing that happened at our house.* New York: Four Winds Press.

Chaback, Elaine; and Fortunato, Pat. 1981. *The official kid's survival kit: How to do things on your own.* Boston: Little, Brown.

Clifton, L. 1975. *My brother fine with me.* New York: Holt, Rinehart, and Winston.

Drescher, Joan. 1981. *I'm in charge.* New York: Atlantic Publishers.

Detrich, S. 1983. *In charge: A complete handbook for kids with working parents.* New York: Alfred Knopf.

Freeman, Lori. 1985. *A kid's guide to first aid: What would you do if. . .* Nashville, Tenn.: School-Age Notes.

Gilbert, Sara. 1983. *By yourself.* New York: Lothrop, Lee, and Shepard Books.

Hubbard, Kate; and Berlin, Evelyn. 1987. *Help yourself to safety: A guide to avoiding dangerous situations with strangers and friends.* Mount Dora, Fla.: KIDSRIGHTS.

Kyte, Kathy. 1983. *In charge: A complete handbook for kids with working parents.* New York: Alfred Knopf.

Long, Lynette. 1984. *The kid's self-care book: On my own.* Washington, D.C.: Acropolis Books.

Long, Thomas. 1985. *Safe at home, safe alone.* Alexandria, Va.: Miles River Press.

Moore, Emily. 1983. *Just my luck.* New York: E.P. Dutton.

Pfafflin, N. 1982. *Survival skills for kids.* Blacksburg, Va.: Polytechnic Institute and State University.

Schick, Eleanor. 1980. *In home alone.* New York: Dial Press.

———. 1982. *Joey on his own.* New York: Dial.

Skurzynski, G. 1979. *Martin by himself.* Boston: Houghton Mifflin.

Stanek, Muriel. 1987. *All alone after school.* Mount Dora, Fla.: KIDSRIGHTS.

Swan, Helen; and Houston, Victoria. 1985. *Alone at home: Self-care for children of working parents.* Englewood Cliffs, N.J.: Prentice-Hall.

The telephoto book: The emergency phone book for kids. Belmont, Calif.: David S. Lake Publishers.

Wolff, Margaret. 1985. *The kid's after-school activity book.* Belmont, Calif.: David S. Lake Publishers.

Assistance Organizations

This section details the major assistance organizations concerned with school-age and home-alone children. Assistance organizations provide such services as dissemination of resources on home-alone and other school-age children, materials for replicating model after-school programs for home-alone youngsters, and other types of technical assistance.

Boys Scouts of America. 1325 Walnut Hill Lane, Irving, Tex. 75062. Publishes training manuals for staff in school-age child care programs and for children in self-care. Its training program, "Prepared for Today," helps children follow safety rules, respond to emergencies, care for younger siblings, plan meals, learn about their neighborhood, and solve problems.

Camp Fire, Inc. 4601 Madison Avenue, Kansas City, Miss. 64112. Has published a self-reliance program for home-alone kids in second through fourth grades. The program is called, "I Can Do It" and is available from Camp Fire.

Center for Early Adolescence. Suite 223, Carr Mill Mall, Carrboro, N.C. 27510. The center disseminates information such as resource lists and bibliographies that deal with school-age and early adolescent children.

Children's Defense Fund. 122 C Street, N.W., Washington, D.C. 20001. Publishes information on prevention problems, issues, and news regarding children of all ages. A newsletter and booklets are available for parents, child advocates, community leaders, public health workers, and others interested in improving the lives of children.

Day Care and Child Development Council of America. 711 Fourteenth Street, N.W., Suite 507, Washington, D.C. 20005. Offers information and technical assistance on all types of day care, including after-school care for school-age youngsters. A newsletter, *Voices for Children,* is also sponsored by the council.

Family Day Care Check-in Project. Fairfax County Office for Children, 11212 Waples Mill Road, Fairfax, Va. 22030. Provides a comprehensive package of materials for those interested in adapting the Family Day Care Check-in Project in their neighborhoods. The package contains step-by-step procedures for starting up, administering, supervising, and evaluating a program. In addition to addressing such issues as licensing, zoning, and liability, the materials include a section on community outreach, describing methods of educating the community about the needs and problems of unsupervised young adolescents.

Girl Scouts of America. 830 Third Avenue, New York, N.Y. 10022. Publishes a training program for children in self-care titled "Safe and Sound at Home Alone."

"I'm in Charge." 7251 West 38th Avenue, Wheat Ridge, Colo. 80033. A course for families to learn about self-care. It is designed for children in fourth through eighth grades and their parents. Parents are informed of the risks of self-care and are given the tools to decide when self-care is right for their child.

National Committee for the Prevention of Child Abuse. 332 South Michigan Avenue, Suite 950, Chicago, Ill. 60604. Involved in school-age child care as part of an overall project to promote the well-being of children. The organization is committed to developing a wide variety of community programs to assist families in supervising their school-age children, rather than favoring only adult-care programs.

National Crime Prevention Council. Woodward Building, 733 Fifteenth Street, N.W., Washington, D.C. 20005. Publishes a kit for safety in self-care. *Keeping kids safe: Kids keeping safe.* The packet includes the *Play it safe* coloring book and topics on babysitting and bicycle safety.

National PTA. 700 North Rush Street, Chicago, Ill. 60611. A professional organization for parents, teachers, and others concerned with bridging the gap between home and school for the welfare of the nation's youth.

PhoneFriend. P.O. Box 735, State College, Pa. 16804. An after-school telephone help line for children at home without adult supervision. The goals of PhoneFriend are to create a helping network to provide information and support for home-alone children after school hours, to help these kids help themselves, and to increase community awareness of the children's needs. A PhoneFriend replication packet giving information and instructions on how to establish and operate a help line for children is available from the above address.

School-Age Child Care Project. Center for Research on Women, Wellesley College, 828 Washington Street, Wellesley, Mass. 02181. A national information and technical assistance resource, committed to promoting the development of programs and services for children between the ages of five and twelve, before and after school at such times when there is a need for care and supervision. Offers technical assistance throughout the country regarding the design and implementation of school-age child care programs, publishes a newsletter, and acts as a clearinghouse for national programs and publications on home-alone kids and school-age child care.

YMCA. 316 Huntington Avenue, Boston, Mass. 02115. In addition to special summer and year-round programs, the YMCA has published a manual, *YMCA School-Age Child Care,* giving information on what kinds of activities should be included in after-school and summer programs.

YWCA. Eastern Seaboard Office, 135 W. 50th Street, 4th Floor, New York, N.Y. 10020. Offers courses for children that will aid them being on their own: water safety, first aid, and survival skills.

Magazines and Newsletters

This section highlights magazines and newsletters that publish articles pertaining to home-alone kids, school-age child care, and elementary school youngsters in general.

Magazines

Child, P.O. Box 11224, Des Moines, Iowa 50347. Published every other month. This magazine's focus is on children's fashion, with occasional relevant topics dealing with child care and family issues.

Children. Rodale Press, 33 E. Minor Street, Emmaus, Pa. 18098. Published bimonthly. This magazine takes a no-nonsense approach to child development with tips for parents on all aspects of child care and child rearing.

Mothers Today, 441 Lexington Avenue, New York, N.Y. 10017. Keeps parents abreast of contemporary issues of motherhood and child rearing.

Parent's Magazine, 685 Third Avenue, New York, N.Y. 10017. Contains articles pertinent to child development and upbringing that will help parents with the many modern-day challenges of child rearing.

Parenting Magazine. Subscription Department, P.O. Box 52424, Boulder, Colo. 80321. Tips for parents on all aspects of child development and child care. We recommend this of all the parenting magazines.

PTA Today, National PTA, Program Department, 700 North Rush Street, Chicago, Ill. 60611. Publishes articles of mutual concern to parents, teachers, and other school personnel. Reprints of numerous articles on home-alone kids and after-school care are available from the above address.

Working Mother, 230 Park Avenue, New York, N.Y. 10169. Published monthly. This magazine helps working women balance their careers, children, and home life.

Working Parents, 441 Lexington Avenue, New York, N.Y. 10017. Aimed at moms and dads, both of whom work and need support in the care and guidance of their children.

Working Woman, 342 Madison Avenue, New York, N.Y. 10173. Designed for career women. Includes a broad range of topics, from hints on achieving the corporate look in dress to the best way to care for your child while pursuing a successful career.

Newsletters

Children's Defense Fund Reports. Children's Defense Fund, 122C Street, N.W., Washington, D.C. 20001. Includes news and issues in federal, state, and local initiatives for children. Monthly.

First Teacher. P.O. Box 29, Bridgeport, Conn. 06602. Designed like a newspaper and filled with excellent activities parents can carry out with their children during quality time. Monthly except July and August.

PhoneFriend Newsletter. PhoneFriend, P.O. Box 735, State College, Pa. 16804. Gives information on new programs, facts, and articles on home-alone issues. Also provides news from other warmlines across the country, and "Phonefriend Childspeak," a column that contains quotes from children's telephone calls. Quarterly.

School-Age Child Care Project Newsletter. Center for Research on Women, Wellesley College, Wellesley, Mass. 02181. Details upcoming national events, important legislation, new publications for parents, and various actions being taken on behalf of school-age children around the country. Three issues a year.

School Age Notes, P.O. Box 120674, Nashville, Tenn. 37212. Provides tips for planning activities and program management for school-age children. Six issues a year.

Voices for Children. Day Care and Child Development Council of America, 711 Fourteenth Street, N.W. Suite 507, Washington, D.C. 20005. The newsletter of the Day Care and Child Development Council of America.

Audiovisuals

The following audiovisuals can be used at PTA meetings or other community meetings to emphasize the importance of support programs for home-alone children. We have organized this section by type of audiovisual.

16mm Films

Better Safe Than Sorry. FilmFair Communications, 10900 Ventura Boulevard, Studio City, Calif. 91604. Presents a series of vignettes on children encountering strangers under potentially dangerous circumstances—for example, when children walk home alone from school or a stranger comes to their door. Dramatized examples are followed by common-sense rules for personal safety and avoidance to match age levels.

Children of Working Mothers. KIDSRIGHTS, 3700 Progress Boulevard, P.O. Box 851, Mount Dora, Fla. 32757. Children praise their wage-earning mothers in this touching program. Using informal group discussions as its format, the insights generated in this twenty-eight-minute film are startling and sensitive at the same time.

In Charge at Home (Latchkey Children). FilmFair Communications, 10900 Ventura Boulevard, Studio City, Calif. 91604. A 1985 release that presents vignettes of children coping on their own at home. Includes what to do if a key is lost, checking in with a parent upon arrival at home, how to answer the door and telephone, and other responsibilities that home-alone children must assume. Also available on videocassette (any size).

Lord of the Locks. Living Center for Family Enrichment, 3515 Broadway, Kansas City, Miss. 64111. A twenty-eight-minute film that highlights the seriousness of self-care and the need for responsible actions by both parent and child. Through two magical characters, the humorous story illustrates possible self-care dangers, the feelings of parents and children, and appropriate child-parent response.

What Ever Happened to Childhood? Churchill Films, 662 North Robertson Boulevard, Los Angeles, Calif. 90060. A forty-five-minute film that portrays the rush children are in to grow up. Highlights home-alone children and their problems. Suggests that childhood as we know it may no longer exist for many children. Interviews older home-alone kids responsible for younger siblings while parents work.

Work and Family: Walking the Tightrope. Bureau of National Affairs, Customer Service, 9435 Key West Avenue, Rockville, Md. 20850. This thirty-minute film explores how employers and unions are responding to the family needs of a new generation of workers. Child care options for working parents, maternity, paternity, adoption-leave policies, alternative work schedules, and assistance programs are discussed.

Videotapes

Children and Working Parents. Education Center of Sheppard Pratt, 6501 North Charles Street, Towson, Md. 21204. A twenty-minute videotape that presents seven parents who discuss their own career circumstances and child care problems after viewing a dramatized home-alone episode. Topics include quality parenting, job demands, and responsibilities. An accompanying packet, "Juggling," contains individual sheets showing self-help skills and solutions for many of the situations raised by the discussion.

Latchkey Families Project. National Television Workshop, 485 Fifth Avenue, Suite 1042, New York, N.Y. 10017. This videotape is an edited version of a two-week series of special television programs reviewing issues faced by home-alone families in Philadelphia. Accompanying the video is a booklet on the project, fact sheets for parents, and a contract for healthy home-alone families. *(3/4 inch)*

Nutrition on the Run: Snacks and Fast Foods. Sunburst Communcations, Room Q 7575, 39 Washington Avenue, Pleasantville, N.Y. 10570. Especially helpful for home-alone kids who prepare their own snacks when in self-care. Encourages teens to question the nutritional quality of the food they buy and eat.

A Parent's Library

This section provides further readings from magazines and other periodicals for parents who wish to read more on the subject of home-alone children.

Barko, N. 1988 April. When school's out: At what age are kids ready to be on their own? *Working Mother,* 79.

Behan, R.A. 1985. Should Johnny or Janet "sit" themselves? *PTA Today, 10,* 27–28.

Chaback, E.; and Fortunato, P. 1983 February. A kid's survival checklist: When you're home alone. *Parents Magazine,* 134–136.

Clements, C. 1983 February. Lessons for latchkey kids. *Ladies Home Journal,* 50.

Conroy, M. 1988 August. After-school programs for kids. *Better Homes and Gardens,* 22.

Grollman, E.A.; and Sweder, G.L. 1986 March. Preparing your child to be home alone. *Working Woman,* 154–156.

———. 1986 February. Tips for working parents from kids. *Reader's Digest,* 107–110.

Hagan, S. 1981. Setting up an after-school program. *Parents Magazine,* 44, 48, 50–54.

Huff, K. 1982 September 20. In their own words. *People Magazine,* 83–84, 87–88.

Iacobucci, K. 1982 May. After-school alternatives for latchkey kids. *McCall's Magazine,* 36.

Kieffer, E. 1981 February 24. The latchkey kids—How are they doing? *Family Circle,* 28–35.

Langway, L. 1981 February 24. The latchkey children. *Newsweek,* 96–97.

Lapinski, S. 1982 September 12. Latchkey blues: When kids come home. *Family Weekly.* 22–23.

Leishman, K. 1980 November. When kids are home alone—How mothers make sure they're safe. *Working Mother,* 21–22, 25.

Levine, J.; and Seltzer, M. 1980 September. Why are these children staying after school? (And why are they so happy about it?) *Redbook Magazine,* 23, 158, 160, 163–166.

Long, L.; and Long, T. 1982 March. What to do when children are home alone. *Essence,* 38–41.

———. 1982 May. The unspoken fears of latchkey kids. *Working Mother,* 88–90.

———. 1982 September 20. The lonely life of latchkey children. *People Magazine,* 63–65.

Munday, M. 1986. Working parents: How to help your latchkey child use time alone responsibly. *PTA Today, 11,* 14–15.

Raymond, B.B. 1985 September. And they said kindergarten would be easier! At least day care lasted the whole day. *Working Mother,* 118–120.

Robinson, B.E. 1986 July. Where do the children go? *Lady's Circle Magazine,* 22–24.

Rodman, H. 1980 July. How children take care of themselves. *Working Mother,* 61–63.

Wellborn, S.N. 1981 September 14. When school kids come home to an empty house. *U.S. News & World Report,* 42, 47.

Whitbread, J. 1979 February 20. Who's taking care of the children? *Family Circle,* 88, 89, 102–103.

Boredom Busters: After-School Activities

No matter what after-school arrangement is used, children get bored from time to time. Helping your child find suitable, constructive, fun outlets is an ever-present challenge. The following boredom busters were written by Sandra Sparks especially for home-alone children. These activities can be selected and adapted to the interest and age of your child and will make the home-alone experience safe and happy and adjustment easier. You can enjoy quality time with your child by providing the materials for the activities and participating in as many as possible.

1. Make a scrapbook. Staple blank paper together to make a book. Then tape or glue in anything that has special meaning to you—souvenirs, postcards, movie tickets, awards, pictures, and so forth.

2. Get a state map and trace the route to some location you think would be fun to visit.

3. Be a pen pal and have fun learning about other people and other places. For possible pen pals write these places: Around the World Friends, 550 Fifth Avenue, New York, New York 10036; American Friends Service Committee, 160 North Fifteenth Street, Philadelphia, Pennsylvania; International Friendship League, 40 Mount Vernon Street, Boston, Massachusetts. Or you can write the United Nations.

4. Try chalk painting. You will need colored chalk, paper towels, and a pan of water. Dip the chalk into the water, and use it to draw anything you want on the dry paper towel. Experiment with different colors and designs. Allow the picture to dry before you hang it up. Have a special place in your house to display your art.

5. Make up a funny song, pantomime, story, or jokes to share with your family at dinner.

6. What's in the future? Design clothes, cars, houses, and so on—whatever you like for the year 2050.

7. Make a bird feeder. Mix bird seed and peanut butter together. Stuff the mixture between the petals of a pine cone. Tie a string or a piece of yarn around the top of the cone to hang it. You can also string raisins and popcorn. When your parents get home from work, you can hang the bird feeders on a tree branch facing a window of your house so you can watch the birds each day.

8. Plan a dinner for the president. What would you serve?

9. Write a story for your favorite television show.

10. Go shopping with a catalog and pretend you have $100 to spend. What would you buy? Would you buy one or two expensive items or many less expensive items? What if you had $500 or $1,000?

11. Make a puppet. Paper bags, an old sock, a mitten, or a glove with yarn hair and button eyes or a painted face works fine. The easiest puppet to make is simply to draw a face on the palm of your hand and wrap a fabric scrap around your hand and arm for a costume.

12. Make a puzzle. Glue a picture from a magazine on a piece of cardboard or posterboard. Let it dry. Use a black ink pen or marker to mark the picture into sections. Cut along the black lines to make the puzzle pieces.

13. Make your own greeting cards. Create messages, verses, and pictures with markers, crayons, or paints on plain or solid-colored paper. Make different sets of cards to give: birthday, get well, thinking-of-you, and so on.

14. "Green Thumb Project." Put a sponge on a dish. Wet the sponge. Sprinkle grass seed on top of the sponge. Wet the sponge a little each day when you get home from school. The seeds should sprout in about one week. For extra fun, have Mom or Dad help you cut the sponge into an animal shape the night before you are going to plant it.

15. Have you got a question for the president or something you would like to tell the president? Write him!

> The President
> The White House
> Washington, D.C. 20500

16. Write and draw pictures for a storybook to share with a younger brother or sister or a neighborhood friend. Maybe you can make up funny endings to nursery rhymes or stories.

17. Try fingerprint art. Press your fingertips down on an ink pad; then press your fingertips on paper. Draw lines and other details to make fingerprints into bugs, monsters, animals, people, and other objects.

18. Write a note, story, secret code, or letter to a friend using typed letters and words cut out of the newspaper. Be careful cutting. Glue or tape the letters and words in the correct order to say what you want them to say. Be sure to use an old newspaper that has already been read.

19. Keep a daily journal. Staple blank sheets of paper together and decorate the cover. Each day write about what happened that day at school or while you were home.

20. Plan the house and yard you would like to have someday. Arrange and glue magazine pictures of houses, trees, flowers, shrubs, and so on on posterboard to show your dream house to friends.

21. Try washcloth painting. Ask permission first. Be sure to do this only on a cabinet or kitchen table top that has a Formica (plastic coating) top. Wet a dark-colored washcloth, and put it on the kitchen table. Run a bar of soap back and forth on the washcloth until it is sudsy. Draw pictures in the suds with your fingers. Smooth over to erase. Remember to rinse the washcloth out in the sink when finished and to dry the table!

22. Pretend you are a radio disc jockey. Make up your own commercials or some ''deejay chatter'' to perform for your family.

23. Draw a picture of an animal, shape, person, or any other item. Glue yarn around the outline of the picture. Then fill in the inside area of the picture with dry beans, popcorn, seeds, cereal, or macaroni, which you glue in place.

24. Pretend you have your own restaurant. Make up your own menu. What would you serve? How much would you charge for your food? What would you name your place?

Index

About the Authors

BRYAN E. ROBINSON is professor of child and family development at the University of North Carolina at Charlotte. He is coauthor of five other books, *Child Development and Relationships, The Developing Father, Latchkey Kids, Teenage Fathers,* and *Working with Children of Alcoholics,* and has published more than fifty articles in professional journals and popular magazines such as *Psychology Today.* Dr. Robinson has been active in research and program development for home-alone kids in Charlotte, N.C. He was project director for the Council for Children's Study of Latchkey Families, helped design and implement school-age child-care programs, and developed videotapes and an activity manual for training school-age child care staff. He has written scripts for national television programs on child development and has appeared on national radio and television discussing children's needs.

BOBBIE H. ROWLAND is professor of child and family development at the University of North Carolina at Charlotte. She is a leader in statewide efforts to provide affordable, quality child care options for children and their parents. Dr. Rowland has conducted research on latchkey children and designed school-age child care training modules and activities for staff. She has developed creative media kits, songs, and stories for young children, and she has written curricula for preschool and elementary-age children for the United Methodist Church. A leader in child advocacy, Dr. Rowland has appeared on national television and in films on issues affecting children. Internationally, Dr. Rowland has worked with family and children programs in the South Pacific, China, the Middle East, Europe, North Africa, Scandinavia, and Greece.

MICK COLEMAN is extension specialist in the Extension Division of the University of Georgia. He received his doctorate from the University of Georgia in child and family development. Dr. Coleman's dissertation dealt with service delivery for latchkey children and their families. He worked extensively with latchkey families in Charlotte, North Carolina, and the Richmond, Virginia, area and helped design school-age child care training modules and activities for staff. Dr. Coleman currently conducts training on school-age child care and latchkey children's issues for the state of Georgia. His other areas of interest include stress management, sports involvement, family functioning, and men's friendships.